Praise for *CALM not BUSY*

Kivi is a master at untangling workplace problems and providing simple tools to keep you CALM. I've finally been able to dig myself out from under the weight of my assignments and breathe again.

—Sharon Sharp, Marketing and
Communications Associate, SPCA Tampa Bay

CALM should be the Myers-Briggs of nonprofit communications. I want to see my peers asking each other, "What's your CALM score?"

—Thomas Negron, Communications Director,
Catskill Animal Sanctuary

I would pay thousands to take back the time and stress I experienced in my starting years because I was unaware of the simple techniques like these that Kivi shares. It's worth its *price* in gold. When I need reassurance, or to feel secure in what I am doing, I seek Kivi's knowledge. This book is no exception, and it did not let me down.

—Anysa L. Holder, Assistant Vice President
of Marketing, Easterseals New Jersey

Kivi has opened my eyes to so many truths about nonprofit communications, and this book is her best yet. It gets to the heart of what keeps us on the hamster wheel and how we can finally jump off. And as always, her clear, direct style makes this an easy yet powerful read.

—Cindy Olnick, Communications Director,
Los Angeles Conservancy

After reading the first three chapters, I was already inspired to re-evaluate how I organize my work and approach my colleagues. *CALM not BUSY* has truly empowered me to be a better (and happier) nonprofit professional.

—Helen Frank, Director of Communications,
NYC Outward Bound Schools

CALM not BUSY helps nonprofit change agents like you and me gain the upper hand on our workload, while refortifying our passion for the work we do. Kivi's approach helped me integrate deliberate planning, thoughtful strategy, and priority setting that empowers me to do the most productive, effective communications work I can in one day. More than just a read, *CALM not BUSY* helps me execute!

—Tara Collins, Director, Communications & Resource Development, RUPCO

Kivi is THE source for making sense of the overwhelming chaos that typically comes with being a nonprofit communicator. I had the opportunity to learn and apply the CALM framework. The concepts have guided further collaboration and understanding between departments, moving towards more effective, focused work.

—Lisa Sherrill, Communications Director, Food Bank of Contra Costa & Solano

Going from BUSY to CALM is a journey of empowerment for communicators at any level. It is building up your strengths, and turning your weaknesses from stumbling blocks to stepping stones.

—Michelle C. Whittaker, Creative Consultant, MCW Creative Group

Kivi is unsurpassed in keeping nonprofit communications leaders on task and sane. She is wise beyond her years, and you need to read her book. She'll be your coach and mentor.

—Jeanine Marlow, Director of Communications & Marketing, Cornerstone Preparatory Academy

High turnover rates are an existential threat to the many societal benefits brought by the nonprofit sector. CALM not BUSY is essential to preventing burnout and increasing impact!

—Steven Shattuck, Chief Engagement Officer, Bloomerang

This is the book I wish I had when I started my nonprofit career! Kivi's wisdom is honest and actionable—and it works.

—Leili Khalessi, Director of Strategic Communications,
American Leadership Forum – Mountain Valley Chapter

Kivi has been an important mentor for me over the years. Her approach is actionable, direct, and aimed at moving the nonprofit communications field forward.

—Sue Clement, Senior Director
Digital Content Strategy, ASPCA

CALM not BUSY

CALM not BUSY

How to Manage Your Nonprofit's Communications for **Great Results**

Kivi Leroux Miller

BOLD & BRIGHT
—— M E D I A ——

Published by Bold & Bright Media, LLC.
319 Becks Church Road
Lexington, North Carolina 27292
Boldandbrightmedia.com

ISBN-13: 978-0692961056
ISBN-10: 0692961054

Library of Congress Control Number: 2017959821

Bold & Bright Media is a multimedia publishing company
committed to bold hearts, bright minds and storytellers whose
experiences will inspire and compel others to grow in their
own greatness. Our first series of publications will focus
on nonprofit guides and compelling storytelling.

Dedication

If you've participated in the Nonprofit Marketing Guide community through our All-Access Training Pass, the Communications Director Mentoring Program, or our Accelerator courses, you've played an essential role in the creation of *CALM not BUSY* and the contents of this book. It's only by exploring your work with you, day in and day out, that I could see the trends in our field. If you've asked a question during a keynote, workshop, or webinar I've presented, you've helped me refine my explanations even further. Thank you.

This book is dedicated to you.

Contents

Preface

For nearly 20 years, I've taught nonprofit staff about communications best practices. My two previous books, *The Nonprofit Marketing Guide* and *Content Marketing for Nonprofits*, are full of marketing, fundraising, and communications advice.

But after training thousands of organizations and personally mentoring more than one hundred communications directors, I've learned that creating good work products isn't enough. What separates the great nonprofit communications teams from the less effective ones is their overall approach to the work and how they build a positive working culture around communications within a nonprofit.

Nonprofit Communications on a Bad Day

A couple of years ago, when I asked friends in the sector what my next book should cover, the consensus was around helping communications directors deal with the hard and often very unpleasant situations that they regularly find themselves in. We labeled these situations the "fusterclucks." Maybe you recognize some of the people who fuel them:

- Managers who avoid planning and decision making for months only to have pages and pages of ideas and criticisms right before launch.
- Overnight experts who read one blog post and suddenly know more about your job than you do.
- Power- and prestige-hungry volunteers and donors who see a path to their own glory . . . right through or over you.
- Coworkers who can't meet a communications deadline but think you're incompetent because you won't instantly whip up a flyer, press release, or viral video on their thing, on the spot.

Nonprofit Communications on a Good Day

If most your days are fusterclucks, it's time to find a new job, because there are many nonprofits where you'll encounter people like these instead:

- Managers who set priorities and who trust and empower their staff to implement them.
- Coworkers who value the role of communications staff in helping them achieve their own work goals and fully cooperate with communications staff to produce shared results.
- Volunteers and board members who plug themselves into an existing communications strategy and take direction from staff as often as they give it, truly acting as a team member.

Getting to More Good Days Than Bad

About the same time as the fusterclucks conversations, Serrie Fung was considering enrolling in Nonprofit Marketing Guide's Communications Director Mentoring Program. She asked me an insightful question: "In a word or two, what did successful participants get out of the program?"

My instant reply was "a sense of calm."

Serrie's question and my response—"calm"—stuck with me for several weeks. I kept going back to my answer and thinking about what I really meant by it. As I explored it, I realized that the word could also be an acronym for the qualities of a good communications director. Thus a "sense of calm" about the communications workload and how to build a culture of communications in the workplace became "CALM: Collaborative, Agile, Logical, and Methodical."

Since then, CALM has become an important component of the Mentoring Program and other training and coaching courses at Nonprofit Marketing Guide. We've conducted additional research that has confirmed and refined the importance of CALM on improving communications effectiveness, building organizational marketing maturity, and increasing job satisfaction.

In other words, CALM reduces the frequency of the fuster-clucks, bringing you many more good days than bad as a nonprofit communications director.

While developing CALM as a model, I continued to explore the daily challenges of nonprofit communications directors, which can be described, in a phrase, as being "too busy." There too I found meaning in the word as an acronym. BUSY stands for "Bogus, Unrealistic, Sidestepping, and Yoked." BUSY is what happens in many nonprofits by default. BUSY is your enemy as a communications director.

CALM is the natural antidote to BUSY. If you want to be more proactive and less reactive, focus on CALM. If you want to be more strategic, and less chaotic, focus on CALM. If you want your communications within your nonprofit to be integrated and aligned with the rest of the organization, rather than an afterthought, focus on CALM.

Ready? Let's explore what CALM looks like and how you can get there.

PART I

Understanding CALM not BUSY

In Part I, we'll define CALM not BUSY and explore some of the consequences of staying BUSY. You'll also take an assessment to get your current CALM score.

What is CALM not BUSY?

What's CALM?	What's BUSY?
C is for Collaborative — It's the WHO. Communications work should always be collaborative in its creation, and in how it is used by your nonprofit to achieve bigger goals.	**B is for Bogus.** It's bogus to think that communications activity is the same thing as communications accomplishments, or that the same activities year after year will somehow produce different results.
A is for Agile — It's the WHEN and WHERE. Communications work requires you to be nimble and constantly adapting the pace and location of communications as needed.	**U is for Unrealistic.** Communications plans and to-do lists often expect far too much, far too quickly, with far too little resources.
L is for Logical — It's the WHAT and WHY. Communications work, even in its most creative forms, should always be clear in purpose and backed by reason.	**S is for Sidestepping.** Communications work must be strategic. But too often, nonprofits avoid making the hard choices about priorities, constantly sidestepping those conversations and decisions.
M is for Methodical — It's the HOW. Communications work should follow clear processes and use tools that improve efficiency.	**Y is for Yoked.** Nonprofit staff can be yoked, or chained, to bad habits and mistaken assumptions that make it harder to get good communications work done.

CHAPTER 1

What BUSY Really Is and Why You Need to Fight It

You are busy, right? So, so busy.

I can relate. I'm busy too. So is everyone else.

Many nonprofit communications directors feel like they work in a constant state of chaos. You might feel worn out because there are simply too many things to do. You likely have too many choices and too many decisions to make on each item on your to-do list, compounding the chaos.

You might feel rudderless. Your boss either doesn't consistently provide strategic direction, changes that direction frequently, or has left you alone to figure it out.

You might feel stuck. The workload isn't going to get better anytime soon. You care about the work, but the job is increasingly frustrating, and you aren't sure how to make it better.

You likely feel overwhelmed and understaffed. Odds are you don't have enough time to think or plan, so you just do, do, do. And the to-dos don't stop coming. Your desk is the dumping ground for every good idea in the organization without an obvious home.

All this busyness is exacerbated by the realities of nonprofit communications work today.

Communications work is fast paced and constantly changing. The job of a nonprofit communications director is so varied from nonprofit to nonprofit that there is no common job description or playbook to follow. Everyone—even those nonprofits that really seem to have their acts together—is making this up as they go.

Confronting all this busyness openly and honestly is hard in the nonprofit sector, where people often feel like they must go above and beyond for the sake of the causes they serve. Staff often feel guilted into working long, hard hours. It creates a lot of martyr-like behavior.

We've Turned Busyness into a Brand

In his 2015 book, *Busy: How to Thrive in a World of Too Much*, Tony Crabbe says we've let our workplaces get this way because it's easier than the alternative. Busyness allows us to avoid tough choices and the important activities that are too hard to be accomplished quickly. Busyness is an addiction, says Crabbe, one that has become a social norm.

He also says that busy has become a personal brand: if we are busy, we must be valuable to the world. Who doesn't want to feel important? Are you sleep deprived? That means you must be super busy, and therefore you are even more important.

In his book, Crabbe points out some undeniable facts that are all too real for nonprofit communicators: it's not your fault that you can't do it all, because there is simply too much to do. You can't control the volume and speed of all the inputs coming at you – email messages, social media updates, office interruptions, even your own good ideas.

While you can't necessarily control other people or your environment, you can control your response to them.

Recognizing Busyness for What It Really Is

When we are more explicit about our busyness and perceived lack of time, what we mean to say is:

- We have too many competing priorities.
- Urgent tasks take precedence over important tasks.
- There are too many interruptions in our work days.

This list is straight from our annual *Nonprofit Communications Trends Reports*. These three problems—not time, per se—are what nonprofit staff say is stopping them from getting their best work done.

At work, we use our busyness to avoid hard conversations, big but important projects, and any kind of change that scares us.

The more you reflect on what busy really means, the more likely you are to see it for what it really is.

Busyness is a lack of leadership in your organization, including your own; bad organizational culture around communications; and bad work habits.

Going along with the busyness is dangerous and self-defeating because the consequences are real for both you and your nonprofit.

BUSY = Bogus, Unrealistic, Sidestepping and Yoked

Let's take a closer look at what BUSY means in the context of nonprofit communications, marketing, and fundraising.

B is for Bogus. Bogus means deceptive, meaningless, or fake.

Measuring your productivity only by your level of activity, not by the result of that activity, is bogus.

Constantly shifting tactics or messaging before any of it has a chance to work is bogus.

Wasting lots of time chasing after quick fixes and silver bullets is bogus.

Thinking your nonprofit and its issues are so unique that no one else can understand or appreciate your challenges is bogus.

U is for Unrealistic. It's unrealistic to expect certain results without adequate time, talent, and resources to produce those results.

Thinking that you can accomplish a mile-long to-do list every day is unrealistic.

Not allowing enough time to get quality, creative work done is unrealistic.

Believing that your nonprofit should be a household name is unrealistic.

Thinking that viral videos are easily manufactured is unrealistic.

S is for Sidestepping. When we avoid making the hard choices about priorities, put off difficult conversations, and shirk other responsibilities, we are sidestepping.

Failing to prioritize what's important, and instead saying all goals are equally important, is sidestepping.

Avoiding hard conversations and failing to say "no" is sidestepping.

Failing to put in the time to really listen to others, internally and externally, is sidestepping.

Allowing walls to build up between departments is sidestepping.

Letting personalities get in the way of collaboration is sidestepping.

Y is for Yoked. We are yoked, or chained, to things and habits that weigh us down and make it harder to get good work done.

Sitting through unnecessary or poorly run meetings yokes you.

Bad assumptions about yourself and others yoke you.

Doing things the same old way without question yokes you.

Responding immediately to every email or social media alert yokes you.

Too many layers of review, too much deliberation on minor details, and perfectionism can yoke you too.

The Consequences of BUSY for You and Your Nonprofit

If you don't minimize BUSY in favor of CALM, both you and your nonprofit will pay a high price.

Here's what happens when you let BUSY rule . . .

- You feel defeated and unmotivated.
- You feel like you are letting others down.
- You feel like a failure.
- All creativity and inspiration are sucked out of you.
- You get resentful toward others.
- You burn out and leave.

Here's what happens to BUSY nonprofits . . .

- They don't get the best out of their staff.
- They miss great opportunities.
- They don't stay relevant within their community.
- They fail to do as much good as they could.

Taking Back Your Work Life

Being CALM not BUSY is about how you choose to use the time, energy, and attention you have available for work. It's about how much control others have over your time, whether because their organizational role grants them that power or because we cede it to them ourselves. It's about treating your time and energy at work as precious commodities.

Personal productivity habits and better planning are important parts of the dynamic, and we'll discuss them in the Methodical section. But they alone won't get you to CALM.

That will require a wholesale shift in how you approach the work, and it takes practice, lots and lots of practice, to stay disciplined.

Busy author Crabbe urges you to:

- Make choices and manage your attention, not just your time.
- Value strategy over productivity.
- Differentiate yourself by thinking creatively and delving into your passions deeply.

Doesn't that sound like a much better way to brand yourself than by always being busy?

· ·

What is This "Team" of Which You Speak?

Throughout the book, we'll refer to the "Communications Team" as the staff who are primarily responsible for communications work. However, we fully understand that many of you reading this book are a team of one, with little to no additional staff time dedicated to communications. That's OK! Virtually everything in the book is easily adapted to work you are doing on your own, or work with other organizational staff, even if they are not officially on the communications team.

· ·

Ready for the Next Step?

Before we move on, it's essential for you to know that you are not alone in the quest for CALM. The challenges you face (and even some of the dysfunction in your nonprofit) are quite common – otherwise I couldn't write a whole book about it!

No one decides to be BUSY. But that's what happens unless you make a conscious decision to be CALM.

Unfortunately, no one is going to fix this for you. You need to fix it yourself, and take control of the BUSY.

This book will help you do that, whether you are managing a team of one—yourself—or a much larger group of people.

Let's start by finding your CALM score.

CHAPTER 2

Getting Your CALM Score

Take the Assessment:
How CALM Are You Now?

Take the 20-question quiz to find your CALM score.

You can also take the most current version of this quiz and get the math done for you online at npmg.us/calmscore.

Answer quickly and honestly using your gut reaction. Don't try to puff up your score or to punish yourself either. This is about helping you identify where you are already making good progress and where some new focus could be helpful.

Answer on a scale of 1-5 for how frequently each statement is true for you:

1 = Never
2 = Rarely
3 = Sometimes
4 = Very Often
5 = Always

#	Statement	My Score (1-5) 1 = never; 5 = always
1	Everything on my to-do list is clearly connected to organizational goals.	
2	I ensure communications decisions are made, and conflicts are resolved, in a thoughtful and timely way.	
3	In the absence of leadership direction on communications, I step up and lead.	
4	I ensure that staff in other departments understand their communications responsibilities and I hold them accountable.	
5	I simplify routines and create repeatable processes to make our communications work easier and more predictable.	
6	I know what our leadership team considers the most important communications priorities from week to week.	
7	I ensure that staff in other departments understand how their specific work fits into our broader communications plan.	
8	I manage the process of creating, reviewing and publishing content so that roles, responsibilities, and deadlines are clear.	
9	I invest time in building a trusting and cooperative relationship with my executive director and/or leadership team.	

10	I regularly and systematically listen to people both inside and outside our organization and keep track of what I learn.	
11	I use every piece of content I create in at least three different ways.	
12	I make progress, no matter how small, on my strategic priorities every day.	
13	I use internal communications tools consistently and facilitate well-run meetings so that others feel included in our communications plans.	
14	I make good communications decisions quickly and those decisions will be trusted and supported by others.	
15	I use an editorial calendar to manage when and where we publish our communications.	
16	I plan for the unexpected so I can react quickly and appropriately when circumstances change or plans go awry.	
17	I say "no" to colleagues when their requests will distract me from communications priorities.	
18	I coach staff through the content creation process so that meeting communications deadlines is less stressful for everyone involved.	
19	I follow best practices, but also experiment freely.	
20	I understand my own productivity style and manage my time and energy well.	

Calculating Your Score

Move the score you gave yourself into this chart, matching up the statement numbers.

For example, for the first statement, if you gave your-self a 3, you would put a 3 in the first block under Logical. If you gave yourself a 5 on the second state-ment, you'd put a 5 in the first block under Collaborative.

Collaborative	Agile	Logical	Methodical
2.	3.	1.	5.
4.	9.	6.	8.
7.	11.	12.	15.
10.	14.	17.	18.
13.	16.	19.	20.
C Total:	A Total:	L Total:	M Total:
Your CALM Score:			

Total your scores for each column. Consider your highest total your top strength.

Then add those four totals together to get your CALM Score.

CHAPTER 3

What Your CALM Score Means and How to Improve It

Getting CALM Will Increase Your Communications Effectiveness

In Nonprofit Marketing Guide's 2017 *Nonprofit Communications Trends Report,* we asked nonprofit communicators to rate their effectiveness in several different ways, including CALM. Organizations that were most effective in implementing the principles of CALM were also most effective by all of the other measures.

When we looked at some of the biggest differences between effective and ineffective nonprofit communications teams, we found that while appropriate staffing and budgets were important, many other top factors were directly related to CALM.

In other words, CALM communications teams are effective communications teams.

The *Nonprofit Communications Trends Reports* reveal that nonprofits are making good progress on several elements of CALM.

For example, most nonprofits said that collaboration within their communications teams, and with fundraising and program staff, got better in 2016. Clarity about communications responsibilities and procedures, and the ability to experiment, also improved in 2016 for about a third of nonprofits.

But we found discouraging trends as well. Over 40% of nonprofits said that focusing on a limited set of priorities, urgent tasks overtaking important ones, and the ability to limit interruptions in their work days all got worse in 2016. Few nonprofits reported improvements in these areas.

How to Interpret Your CALM Score and Where to Begin

Let's first look at your total CALM Score.

If your score is . . .	
49 or less	Many CALM approaches will be new to you. Don't be afraid or overwhelmed, as you have so much to gain! Every positive change you make will be a big step toward CALM not BUSY.
50 - 69	You've dabbled in CALM, but now it's time to make these approaches a more integral part of your work life. Fully embrace and commit to a few CALM concepts.
70 - 89	You work in a CALM way regularly. Keep practicing, refining, and institutionalizing your approaches.
90 or higher	Congratulations! You are a master of CALM. Pass this book on to someone who needs it more than you do and coach them on your CALM ways.

Now what? First, don't get overwhelmed. Take the path to CALM step by step. It's a big "U for Unrealistic" to think you can change your scores overnight.

But which letter do you work on first? That depends on your personality. Would you rather build on your top strength or tackle your biggest weakness?

I am a "build on your strengths" person, so if you aren't sure, start there. On which letters did you score the highest? I suggest firming those up even more (if possible). That's a great base on which to pursue work on the other letters.

If your top score is on Collaborative . . .

Your top strength is being collaborative. You focus on the "who." You know that great communications work depends on strong personal relationships and partnerships with others.

Build on this strength by focusing here:

- Help staff see the big picture of your communications work and how their work fits into it.
- Talk frequently with staff about your communications plan, including holding editorial meetings.
- Build listening and documenting what you hear, internally and externally, into your regular routine.
- Help staff in other departments understand their communications responsibilities and hold them accountable.
- Work through how communications decisions will be made, who will be included in those decisions, and how to resolve conflicts.

If your top score is on Agile . . .

Your top strength is being agile. You focus on the "when and where." You know that great communications work requires you to adapt to constant change and to perform well under pressure.

Build on this strength by focusing here:

- Build an exceptional and trusting relationship with your executive director, leadership team, and other staff members.
- In the absence of leadership, take charge yourself.
- Develop "simple rules" that help you make decisions more quickly.
- Expect the unexpected, and plan for it.
- Create agile content that you can use and repurpose in many ways.

If your top score is on Logical . . .

Your top strength is being logical. You focus on the "why." You know that great communications work demands that you stay focused and grounded.

Build on this strength by focusing here:

- Choose communications goals that are well-integrated with other organizational goals.
- Watch for shifting short-term priorities, but maintain your long-term focus.
- Practice saying "no" in several different ways so your to-do list doesn't grow uncontrollably.
- Follow communications best practices, but experiment freely.
- Track and measure toward your long-term goals, making a little bit of progress every day.

If your top score is on Methodical . . .

Your top strength is being methodical. You focus on the "how." You know that great communications work comes faster and easier when you follow a good routine and work through challenges step by step.

Build on this strength by focusing here:

- Use an editorial calendar, even if you are the only one looking at it.
- Establish content creation, review and publication processes for working with others, including roles and deadlines.
- Build an office culture that understands that timeliness and meeting deadlines are essential to excellent communications.
- Simplify your work routines with formulas and "simple rules" that make your work processes easier.
- Understand your own productivity style and how to best manage your own time and energy.

In Part 2, let's look at each letter in CALM much more closely.

PART 2

Be More Collaborative

C is for Collaborative. It's the WHO of your communications work.

Communications work should always be collaborative in its creation and in how it is used by your nonprofit to achieve bigger goals. Great communications work depends on strong personal relationships and partnerships. Even if you manage your nonprofit's communications by yourself, your larger organization is a team that requires your constant collaboration.

When You Are Collaborative . . .	When You Aren't Collaborative . . .
You are interested in what others in your organization are doing, and you regularly seek them out.	You keep your head down and your butt in your seat. You are isolated from the work of the organization and from decision making.
Time spent with other staff and managers is engaging and worthwhile, rather than a slog of unproductive meetings.	You may feel like you are solely responsible for all of the organization's communications and stuck in a vacuum.
Program staff understand the strategic role that communications plays in helping them achieve their own goals, so they seek out your help and want to help you be successful too.	Staff in your organization don't help out with communications in part because they don't understand their role in it or why it matters.
You welcome discussion and debate, work with others to make good communications decisions, and help resolve inevitable conflicts.	Program staff avoid working with the communications team because the process seems slow, restrictive, or irrelevant.
Creative ideas and opportunities freely flow from lots of places, but you have processes in place so only the best ideas move forward.	You get stuck in a rut and fail to see great opportunities because you lack a broader perspective.

Why Being Collaborative is So Important

Communications directors are the translators and bridges between the people doing the work (inside the nonprofit) and the people supporting and benefitting from that work (outside the nonprofit). All of these people have an important stake and say in what happens, and as a communications director, you are the default "listener in chief" at your nonprofit. You then work with others to take all that you hear and convert it into communications. You collaborate with many different people, every day, as you create, approve, and publish content.

But to maximize that kind of collaboration, you need a high functioning team. Genuine teamwork is hard to achieve, and without a concerted effort, organizations can easily fall into the dysfunctional traps described in the classic management fable and guide, *The Five Dysfunctions of a Team.* In his book, Patrick Lencioni describes a series of cascading problems.

The **absence of trust** within a team, and specifically an unwillingness among team members to be genuinely open and vulnerable with each other, is the first dysfunction.

This leads to the second, which is **fear of conflict**. Veiled discussions and guarded comments are more common than passionate debate.

This lack of healthy debate and discussion results in **lack of commitment**. If team members can't openly share their opinions, they won't fully buy into decisions, even if they pretend they have.

Failing to commit leads to **avoidance of accountability**. Team members don't hold themselves or each other accountable for getting the work done.

Without accountability, there's **inattention to results.** Individuals put their own desires and perceived priorities above the needs of the team and the organization as a whole.

To be collaborative, you need to be aware of these dysfunctions within your organization and do your part to correct them. You'll find advice on how to do that not only in this section on Collaboration, but in the sections on being Agile, Logical, and Methodical too.

In each of the six chapters in Part 2, you'll explore a proven way for communications staff to be more collaborative, including with staff with limited or no direct communications responsibilities.

CHAPTER 4

Connect the Dots Between Your Work and Theirs

I f you want anyone to do anything, that person must see what's in it for them. Sometimes this is very transactional: I'll scratch your back if you scratch mine.

But more often, especially in nonprofit work, the rewards of being collaborative and cooperative are emotional. We can feel good about ourselves when we help someone else. If, as a communications team, you can help program staff feel more productive, accomplished, and personally satisfied with their own work, they are much more likely to cooperate with you.

Putting your communications work in the context of the program work and vice versa is an incredibly important milestone in the marketing maturity of an organization. You must clearly connect the dots between communications, fundraising, and program work.

One simple way to start these conversations is through some show-and-tell that connects the work of different staff. For example,

Diane Hill, development and communications officer of United Community Ministries of Alexandria, Virginia, has developed a list of questions for program staff to ask clients about their experiences before and after coming to the agency for social service help. Using the answers to those questions, program staff can tell Diane a story about the client.

"I then create a handout with the basic story as Exhibit A and then show the program staff Exhibit B, which is the direct mail appeal letter the fundraising and communications staff crafted based on that story," says Diane. "This educates program staff on how we can use their experience with clients to get more funds to enrich and expand their programs."

Create a Big Picture Communications Timeline

It may take a few hours, but another relatively easy place to start is with the *Big Picture Communications Timeline* exercise. I do this all the time with clients and it always opens people's eyes. Every time we do it, you see light bulbs going off over everyone's heads as they finally realize how their little piece of the puzzle fits into the larger communications plan and how interconnected all the pieces are.

This is best done on a big whiteboard, but you can also do it with several big sheets of flipchart paper laid end to end, or a big roll of butcher paper. Give yourself at least six feet. This really does work best if done offline first. Once you are done editing, you can move it online, but I've found just posting pictures of the written timeline works just as well.

Since this is a timeline, pick your starting and ending points. A year, with tick marks for each month, is a good place to start, but if another time range makes more sense for your organization, use that.

Here's what you plot out on that timeline.

Big Events, Outside Your Organization's Control

Look at the calendar that your organization, your participants, your supporters, and the rest of the world are living with. What holidays, seasonal events, or other regular occurrences have a big effect on your communications?

For organizations that do political advocacy, the election cycle is often important, so you'd put down filing deadlines and primary and general election dates. For animal shelters, the start of kitten season, when stray cats start to have their litters, is mid-spring (most kittens are born between April and October).

Food banks benefit from lots of food drives in November and December, but the shelves are often bare during the summer when the people who typically organize food drives (including schools) are busy with vacation plans. Nonprofits that offer after-school sports would chart the season openers and championships for the different sports leagues they play in.

Big Events, Within Your Organization's Control

Next, add the big events that are within your control. Start with events that you host, including everything from annual fundraisers, workshops or conferences, member meetings, major performances, and lobby days. Then add on similar types of events that others host but that you co-sponsor or otherwise participate in in a major way. I'm not talking about events that one of your staff members might attend as professional development, but those events that your whole organization is involved with as a core part of what you do.

Your Major Call-to-Action Campaigns

When are you focused on asking other people to do things? When are you actively asking for donations, such as your year-end campaigns or membership drives? When are you asking people to sign up for a conference or to RSVP for a fundraising event? Think about your programmatic deadlines and milestones. Chart out the time periods when you are focused on asking people to take various actions.

Your Major Story Arcs

Now, layer on the major story arcs within your organization, roughly approximating when they happen. These are the major stories that play out as you deliver your programs and services. These are often tied to events or calls to action you already have on the calendar now, so start there. Try to map out the beginning, middle, and end of those story arcs.

For example, let's say a Friends of the Library group holds an annual used book sale in the May. While they will have already marked the sale weekend on the calendar above, now it's time to build out the story around the book sale. If you treat the book sale as the end of the story, asking the community for donations of used books in February and March (which should be included as a call to action) could be the beginning of the story, and sorting and organizing the books in April could be the middle.

Or, you could treat the book sale (or any other fundraiser) as the beginning of the story, since the money raised there is probably being used for upcoming programming. In this case, the end of story might be a new Story Hour Series in the fall. The middle of the story, in the summer, could be the selection of books, authors, and activities for the series.

With these big milestones, calls to action, and stories in place, it's now much easier to start breaking down this big picture into smaller chunks of time, like a quarter or a month, and to develop a more specific editorial calendar from there. We'll talk more about editorial calendars in the **Methodical** section.

The hardest part of this exercise is often scheduling a couple of hours where you can get program staff, fundraisers, marketers, and executives in the same room. Once you do, you begin to map out on a large timeline of the year all of the major events and milestones (both within and beyond your control) that will drive your communications in the coming year. Then you add on elements like your primary calls to action and the major story lines you want to share.

Going through these and other exercises will help staff see the relevance of communications work to their own success. That's the first step toward more collaboration.

CHAPTER 5

Lead the Internal Conversations about Your Communications Plan

Many of the surprises that upend a communications director's day aren't surprises at all to other people on staff. You just didn't know about it. If this happens a lot, it's time to explore better collaboration and information sharing with your executive team or program staff – or wherever those surprises seem to originate from.

This doesn't necessarily mean you have to create another meeting. But maybe it means you should be sitting in on an existing meeting. Or maybe it just means spending more time with your coworkers so you can check in more informally.

Collaboration doesn't mean that you are always available either, or that you have to respond positively to every request for your time. But it does require a more open flow of internal communications than exists in many nonprofits.

Consistently using internal communications channels, starting new projects with creative briefs, and running productive meetings are all great habits to embrace as you collaborate on your communications work.

Pick the Right Internal
Communications Tool for the Message

It's important to establish cultural norms within your team and the broader organization for what level of communication an issue or question requires. What's instant message-worthy, what's email-worthy, and what's phone, video or in-person meeting-worthy at your organization?

Instant messaging allows you to share quickly and concisely. It's great for status check-ins, reminders, quick questions, and time-sensitive conversations. But don't abuse it. It's also not good for sensitive conversations where tone is important, such as emotional messages or bad news. Some organizations limit its use to content that is both urgent and important. That may be a bit too strident, but it's worth discussing what's appropriate and what's not.

Email is good for information that is purely informational, for progress reports, and for background information. It's not great for information or questions that are especially time-sensitive because those messages can be buried in the "FYI" and less urgent content.

Good old fashioned phone calls are great for time-sensitive information, assuming that you have both caller ID and voicemail. They are also good for complex or sensitive topics that will require some back and forth, or if you suspect you will have multiple follow-up questions. Phone conversations are typically not recorded or archived, which has both advantages and disadvantages.

In-person or video meetings allow for longer, more substantive discussions, debates, brainstorming, and decision making. But they require active participation from multiple people to be successful.

Creative Briefs: Get Answers to Your Questions Upfront

A creative brief is a quick worksheet that you fill out before you get started on any significant piece of communications work. Using a creative brief forces you to consider important questions before you get started. It's also a wonderful collaboration tool that helps your team work out potential conflicts before you spend a lot of time on the project. It's also a nice touchstone that you can return to if you feel like a project is going astray at any point.

I've seen many different versions, but here are the questions you'll usually want to include in one way or another.

- What is it? What is the deliverable?
- What is the goal or purpose of the communications piece?
- What is the single most important thing it should communicate?
- Who is the communications piece for (specific participant or supporter groups, for example)?
- What is the specific call to action?
- Is there a specific voice, tone, or style for this piece that should be reflected in copy or design?
- What gap is this piece filling in our existing communications line-up?
- How will success of the piece be measured?
- Who is the primary decision maker on this piece? Who else is working on it?
- What budget and additional resources will be made available?
- What are the deadlines for the first, intermediate, and final drafts?

Asking staff to complete a creative brief when they need publications or website updates can be a big help to your communications team and to the staff requesting your help. "By using a creative brief, the majority of the information we need is in one place, and it makes the person requesting support think through what they are actually requesting," says Jeanine Marlow, director of communications and marketing for Cornerstone Prep in Acworth, Georgia. "It helps all us feel we are on the same team." The creative brief can also be used, as is or with some relevant adjustment, to brief contractors like freelance graphic designers and copywriters.

Get What You Need Out of Meetings

Bad meetings waste everyone's time. No one wants to sit through a document being read to them. Nor do people want to rehash the to-do list from the last meeting or do work in the meeting that was supposed to be done *before* the meeting.

But meetings aren't all bad. They are a great tool for collaboration when used well. Here are a few meeting basics, regardless of what you are meeting about:

Include the expected outcomes on your agenda. Everyone needs to know what the meeting is about, and just as importantly, what they are expected to do during the meeting. Will you be brainstorming options or making a decision, or both? What information are people expected to have with them during the meeting? What will happen next after this meeting?

Schedule the meeting for the right amount of time. Most meetings are too long, especially if you schedule them for an hour by default. Think in terms of 15-minute chunks of time instead. Many check-in meetings should only be 15 minutes. Others might need two or three hours. Think it through, rather than defaulting to an hour.

During the meeting, work out what happens next. If you will be making task assignments during a meeting, open up a project management tool and get those to-dos recorded during the meeting. If someone is responsible for taking notes or creating a summary, they should do it immediately after the meeting, and get clarity on any key decisions or points with participants before they leave the room. If nothing new will happen after this meeting, odds are you don't actually need the meeting!

The Types of Meetings Communications Directors Need

As a communications director, you need to ensure that several different kinds of meetings are taking place at your organization so that you can do your best work.

Strategic Direction Meetings. These are the "why" and "vision" meetings. During these meetings, which are ideally both annual and quarterly, managers should share the longer-term view of the organization's work. For example, which programs are rising or falling in importance over the next several months? One good tool for this kind of meeting is a *Big Picture Communications Timeline*. The meeting outcome for a communications director is the ability to forecast any needed shifts in communications strategy or messaging.

Scoping Meetings. These are "what" and "who" meetings. You hold these meetings when you are starting something new or trying to flesh out an idea. You can use a creative brief to guide the meeting, or even ask that the creative brief be submitted prior to the meeting.

They are also good for sketching out your editorial calendar three to six months in advance. These meetings are about getting ideas, information, concerns, and insights out on the table and shared among team members. The outcome for the communications director is a clear understanding of the assignment, the resources available, the roles of different staff members in doing the work, etc. You should leave these meetings with a clear set of next steps assigned, using a roles and responsibilities model like those described in Chapter 7.

Content Collection Meetings. During these meetings, or portions of meetings, your goal is to collect the content you need from others. This often includes time for storytelling, for updating evergreen content with new information, and for last-minute timely changes to content.

Cheryl Megurdichian, director of development and communications at Second Sense in Chicago, Illinois, says that incorporating story collection into staff meetings is essential. "Each staff meeting has time set aside for each staff member to share stories of challenges and successes," says Cheryl. "A story can start small, but often multiple staff members work with the same client and the story builds. That generates even more story ideas."

Accountability or Progress Meetings. These are the "how" and "when" meetings and include your typical weekly or monthly editorial meetings as well as most project-specific meetings. You hold these meetings to ensure that work is progressing in a timely way and that team members remain accountable. Use them to share progress, to celebrate successes, to address changing circumstances, to pose and answer questions, and to troubleshoot any issues that come up. You'll often use these meetings to prioritize tasks when too much is going on. That means adjusting assignments and schedules as needed. Keep that project management tool open during the meeting!

These are also good meetings for debriefs after a campaign or project ends. You can discuss what went well, what didn't, changes to the work processes, and other lessons learned as you review the results.

These can be 10-minute daily meetings or hour-long weekly meetings. It just depends on what works best for your organization.

Beware: these are not just "status report" meetings. If everything is going smoothly, focus on what needs to happen next and ensuring that those tasks will be accomplished on time—or end the meeting early and get back to your priorities!

Decision Meetings. While you can make decisions in scoping and accountability meetings, sometimes you need a special meeting where options can be laid out and discussed as a group so that a final decision can be made. These meetings require a good deal of preparation so that the choices are described well and it's clear how the decision will be made (e.g., executive decision, voting, consensus).

Professional Development Meetings. These meetings are used for cross-training staff and practicing new skills. Think about what you need to learn from program or fundraising staff and what you'd like to coach them on as well. Topics might include the elements of a good story or writing for different audiences, for example. "Lunch and Learns" are a popular format for these meetings in the nonprofit sector.

If the kind of internal collaborative conversations described in this chapter are not regularly taking place at your organization, take responsibility for making them happen more often.

CHAPTER 6

Listen to Ideas and Manage What You Hear

"Listener in chief" is a great informal title for communications directors. If you do your job well, you are listening inside your organization for what people want to communicate to the outside world. You are also listening externally to what people outside want to hear from your organization. It's your job to find the nexus of the two.

Go Where Your Coworkers Are; Don't Expect Them to Come to You

Listening internally is not just sitting passively in meetings. It's about actively seeking out your coworkers, talking with them about their work, and observing what they do.

When the Information Services Department of the Bosler Memorial Library in Carlisle, Pennsylvania undertook a rebranding campaign, community relations coordinator Vallie Edenbo visited with staff in all of the library's different departments. "I went to the visits with a list of questions that we could discuss in our downtime, but I went in with an open mind to observe their interactions with the public and to learn about their work first hand," says Vallie. "The visits gave me a sense of their style and the value of their services to a variety of audiences." Vallie and her team eventually built a campaign based on delivering messages to those audiences she observed during her visits.

The library also formed a Marketing and Public Relations Committee that meets monthly. Vallie sits on the committee along with the executive director, development officer, youth services director, and public services director. Each person on the committee brings ideas from their own experience with programs, fundraising, and community outreach. "The team offers a sounding board for new communications ideas, constructive criticisms as needed, and collaboration that helps many of our communications team projects feel like organization-wide efforts," says Vallie.

Being amongst program staff was so important to Tracy Hutchinson Wallace, the communications officer for Habitat for Humanity Trinidad and Tobago in San Juan, that when her office relocated last year, she made a special request. "I deliberately asked for the cubicle closest to the staff room and bathrooms," says Tracy. "Everyone has to walk past me at least once a day, so eventually I am updated informally on all projects." However, she doesn't allow these casual conversations to substitute for a work assignment process. "Formal requests for communications support are only accepted via email," says Tracy.

Leave the Office to Connect with the People You Are Communicating With

Diane Hill's experience as a development and communications coordinator for United Community Ministries of Alexandria,

Virginia is the same with people outside the organization: nothing replaces development and communications staff being on site or at an event in person. Program staff do not have the time or skill to know what makes a good photo or a good story, says Diane. "We position ourselves as a resource to help the program staff make their program work or event a success. We've established our credibility with the program staff," she says.

Nita Wilkinson, the director of advancement for Green Hills Community in West Liberty, Ohio knew she needed to get out into the community more. She says she spent two years talking about it, but not doing it. "Finally, I told my CEO that I was putting it in my fund development plan to be out of the office every Wednesday. I try to make appointments with donors then, although flexibility is important and I meet with them on their schedule. But suggesting Wednesday first is a step," says Nita.

If she doesn't have an appointment scheduled, Nita will set up in a local coffee shop. "It is amazing how many people wander through who you can chat with a bit," says Nita. One day, for example, a "founding father" of her organization walked in. "I had been trying to get an appointment with him, as he hadn't given in many years. We made an appointment right then and there. It was all because I chose to be intentional in getting out of the office every Wednesday and put it into my fund development plan," says Nita.

Create a Holding Pen or Parking Lot, Rather Than Relying on Memory

One outcome of your work toward more collaboration will be a plethora of ideas, suggestions, and criticisms from many places. This is a good thing – if you can manage it well. If you're good at listening, you'll be collecting more ideas for your work than you know what to do with. Whether those good ideas come flowing in from program staff, board members, your visionary leaders, people outside your organization, or your own mind, you need a process to manage them. Don't just immediately start working on every bright idea that comes your way, no matter its source!

You are probably familiar with the idea of holding pens or parking lots from facilitated meetings. If someone comes up with a tangential idea, the meeting facilitator will often write it down on a flip chart labeled "parking lot" so the idea isn't lost, but doesn't sidetrack the meeting agenda.

You want to do the same thing with your ideas for new projects, campaigns, or pieces of content. You don't want to lose them, but you don't want them to derail your current communications plan either.

If the ideas are mostly related to your editorial calendar, I suggest that you use the same system for your holding pen. If you use Excel, create a separate tab. Create a separate board in Trello or a new project in Asana, with each idea as a new task. Or if you organize your content in stages, make Holding Pen the first one, followed by Assigned, Draft, Review, Approve, Published, etc.

You could also create two different sections, like short-term parking and long-term parking, based on either (1) how quickly the idea might come into play or (2) how big or strategic the idea is.

Should you add deadlines or assign ideas to someone at this point? Probably not.

Create a Process to Review the Holding Pen

On some kind of regular schedule (monthly? quarterly?), review everything in your holding pen.

Delete the ideas that have definitely lost their luster or are no longer relevant. Don't feel bad about killing off good ideas! You can't do it all. The more strategic you are, the more ideas you will kill off.

If something still seems like a good idea, but perhaps it's not quite ripe, now is a good time to assign someone to review it again at a certain date.

If you think an idea is ready, start working it through the process you'll create in the next step.

If you aren't sure what to do with it, get some feedback from someone else. Maybe someone else is willing to breathe some life into it.

Don't let ideas linger too long or carry over from month to month indefinitely. At some point, they need to be deleted or worked on.

Create a Checklist to Get Out of the Holding Pen

How does a good idea mature into a task that actually makes it onto your to-do list? You need some criteria!

Understanding how the idea helps you meet an important goal is an essential first step.

But then what?

For example, you could require that you have answers to the three Quick and Dirty Marketing Plan questions: Who are we communicating with? What's the message? How are we delivering that message to those people?

You could also ask the person who came up with the idea to help you complete a creative brief (see Chapter 5).

Remember, you are already working hard. If you add this new idea to your list, that means something else will be a lower priority. Is this new idea that important AND that urgent? What's falling off or down the list as a result of this new idea going on it?

You might also choose to run a test or experiment with the idea to see if it will really work or not before investing too much time or energy.

Actively listening to people both inside and outside of your nonprofit is essential to collaboration and an important part of your job as a communications director. But it's just as important that you actively manage what you hear and thoughtfully incorporate it—or not—into your communications work.

CHAPTER 7

Empower Staff Participation and Insist on Accountability

Even if you are a communications team of one, you can't do good communications work alone. You need the input, feedback, and cooperation of others in your organization.

Building a communications culture that holds everyone in the organization responsible for communications work in some way is vital, and even more important if you are the sole communications staffer.

Communications work has many moving parts and if one of those parts fails, it can bring the whole machine to a grinding halt. Public accountability helps team members—on and off the communications team itself—understand the roles they play and how interdependent and important they are to the organization's communications success. Team members won't want to let each other down.

Assign Responsibilities for Communications Work

You can get clarity on important elements of your work processes, like who needs to be consulted and who has the final decision, using a simple roles and responsibilities framework.

One popular model is RACI.

R = Responsible for the project. This person is the one doing the work.

A = Accountable for the project. This person has the final say.

C = Consulted. This person has information or resources needed by "R" to complete the work.

I = Informed. This person needs to know the project is taking place and when it is completed but does not need to be involved in its creation or approval.

Each person on the team is assigned a letter to indicate their role related to the project as a whole, or to individual tasks, depending on how you organize the work.

Every task should have one and only one R. If you find yourself assigning more than one R per task, you should break down the task even further.

I personally find RACI a little confusing, because I am prone to mixing up "responsible" and "accountable" and also blending "consulted" and "informed."

So I came up with a modified version that makes more sense to me in the nonprofit communications world. It's easy to remember too, because it also spells out CALM: Contributes, Approves, Leads, and Monitors.

C = Contributes. This person helps the Lead with information, resources, or other assistance. They are expected to contribute to getting the work done and communicate clearly with the Lead.

A = Approves. This person approves the final product and perhaps interim drafts as needed. They may also do a final proofread or edit content for tone or style. The Approver should be involved early in scoping out the project (e.g. approving the creative brief) and updated as needed to ensure there are no surprises at final approval time.

L = Leads. This person is primarily responsible for the project and making sure the work gets done. They track all the moving parts, ensures deadlines are met, do much of the actual work, and take interim decisions to the Approver.

M = Monitors. This person should be kept informed about overall progress and when the work is completed but isn't responsible for the work in any substantive way.

Let's apply this model to publishing an email newsletter.

Let's say you have a two-person team with a communications coordinator and a marketing director. The coordinator is the Lead on the newsletter. They work with program staff who are Contributors for that particular edition to draft articles about their projects. They then edit those articles and get the newsletter formatted. The director is the Approver, and they do a final edit before handing it back over to the Lead to publish the newsletter. Program managers whose topics aren't in this edition of the newsletter would be Monitors. They need to know what's in this issue and when it's available but don't need to be involved otherwise.

Look for opportunities to reinforce responsibility and accountability all around you. "We try to ask the question, 'Who else needs to know this?' at the end of meetings and then make someone responsible for sharing," says Julie Bornhoeft, the chief development and marketing officer for WEAVE in Sacramento, California.

"It's not perfect by any means, but consciously thinking about who else is impacted by information" supports a good office culture around communications.

Encourage Staff to Contribute to Communications: Start with Photography

Before social media, nonprofit communicators needed mostly text, and convincing non-communications staff to devote time and energy into writing was (and still is) a challenge.

Now, communicators need visuals as much as they need text. With the proliferation of smartphones with good cameras, it's easier than ever for everyone on staff, regardless of writing talents or interests, to contribute to your nonprofit's communications channels.

Scarlett Bauman, director of marketing for Air Force Enlisted Village, a senior living community in Shalimar, Florida, relies on activities coordinators, community directors, and maintenance supervisors to send her photos. She created a "photography tips sheet" with procedures for submitting to her up to five of the best photos with descriptions whenever they are participating in something that others might enjoy seeing. "Staff have emailed and texted me photos after hours, on weekends, or when I'm on paid time off," says Scarlett. "I can create a social media post from anywhere with my phone so our Facebook page is always current."

Scarlett says it took awhile to get everyone on board, but investing time in building good relationships with everyone she works with has paid off. "Now when I need something, they're happy to cooperate," she says.

Scarlett also relies on the residents themselves to contribute content. "I'm Facebook friends with some of our residents. They like to post photos from their activities and daily life, so if I see something I like, I always ask permission to share their photos on the Air Force Enlisted Village Facebook page," says Scarlett.

Julie Edwards, executive director of the Humane Society of Northeast Georgia in Gainesville, Georgia, agrees that contributing photography is an excellent way for program staff to fulfill their communications responsibilities. "We highly encourage all staff to take 'candids' and forward them to the marketing team," says Julie. "As the marketing team has received and posted these photos, the staff have seen that their contributions are important and impactful which, in turn, continues to turn the wheel."

Julie says the marketing team has also developed great relationships with the shelter's clinical team, and adoption and intake coordinators. "They give us a heads-up when there is a great story to cover," says Julie, rather than waiting for the marketing team to come looking for stories after the fact.

Provide Templates, Samples, and Approved Content for Staff to Use

Another way you can encourage both participation and accountability for communications work—without being directly involved at every step yourself—is setting coworkers up with access to approved templates.

Templates that others can use are a great tool to kick-start a smooth content and review process. (We'll discuss your content review and approval process more in Chapter 23.)

"Using templates keeps the look and feel (and often the basic narrative) consistent, so anyone can create simple documents," says Tracy Hutchinson Wallace, the communications officer for

Habitat for Humanity Trinidad and Tobago in San Juan. She makes all core documents available to staff in Dropbox and Google Apps, including FAQs, profiles, forms, videos, photos, annual reports, and newsletters. Staff also get cheat sheets on the organization's branding guidelines with samples of the narrative, brand platform and language do's and dont's. While everything still goes through Tracy for quality assurance before it leaves the building, someone else can be the "Lead" on the work, while Tracy is in the role of "Approver."

Reward Cooperative Staff Who Follow Through

Tara Collins, director of communications and resource development at RUPCO in Kingston, New York, uses her allotted time at every staff meeting to encourage staff to help her with the organization's communications. "I share 'Grab, Grin & Go Awards' (which are $10 gift certificates) with one to three people who have shared photos or stories, or helped created well-branded pieces for their departments the previous month," says Tara. She then shows how the content was actually used, such as in a brochure or event invitation.

"Instead of begging each month for support, staff are voluntarily responding to this reward program, which is helping me secure content from an otherwise-resistant staff of 65 people," says Tara, who notes that at a cost of just $30/month, she is still well below what it would cost to hire a photographer or graphic designer. "I cheerlead our staff, encouraging them to be the best ambassadors," says Tara, "and a little bribery helps along the way."

With a little creativity and your commitment to building relationships with staff, encouraging others to share the responsibility for, and to collaborate on, your nonprofit's communications can result in wonderful work products and a greater sense of CALM for everyone involved.

CHAPTER 8

Work Through How Communications Decisions Will Be Made

Patrick Lencioni wisely points out in *The Five Dysfunctions of a Team: A Leadership Fable* that two of the greatest causes for lack of commitment to a project are the desire for consensus and the need for certainty. We often see these two factors hurting the chances for successful collaborations in nonprofit communications.

Think about what's slowing down your communications plan, or the decision making needed to implement it, and you'll often realize it's one of those two things or both.

Consensus culture is common in the nonprofit sector, but it can be dangerous to good communications. As Seth Godin once said, "Nothing is what happens when everyone has to agree."

Good communications work requires speed and agility, and on many days, a certain level of risk taking. Consensus, on the other hand, does not work well when rushed and tends to produce more conservative or middle-of-the-road outcomes.

One of the hallmarks of great communications work is a willingness to experiment. However, nonprofits that rely on consensus for these decisions often make compromises with people in the group who are pessimistic or ill-informed or who simply enjoy playing the devil's advocate. You can end up with decisions that everyone is lukewarm about, and therefore no one is committed to pursuing.

That's not to say that naysayers and conflict aren't welcome: conflict is essential to good collaborative processes. You want to hear a variety of opinions and perspectives. You want to gather information from different sources. The difference is how the decision is made – and it must be made.

One common outcome of consensus processes is no decision, often because of the need for certainty. More cautious members of a team may refuse to give their blessings without assurances that are simply impossible to guarantee. Communications work is by nature constantly changing. Yet it's far better to decide, to move forward, and to adjust as needed than it is to make no decision at all or to waffle.

I really appreciated the decision-making advice that Jeff Bezos shared in his 2017 annual letter to Amazon shareholders.

Bezos says "most decisions should probably be made with somewhere around 70% of the information you wish you had." Waiting for more certainty will make you too slow. He also points out that you need to be good at quickly recognizing and correcting bad decisions anyway. So if you're good at course correcting, being wrong is less costly than you think. Being slow definitely costs you.

Bezos also recommends the phrase "disagree and commit." He says, "If you have conviction on a particular direction even though there's no consensus, it's helpful to say, 'Look, I know we disagree on this but will you gamble with me on it? Disagree and commit?' By the time you're at this point, no one can know the answer for sure, and you'll probably get a quick yes."

Collaboration on an outstanding nonprofit communications plan requires communicating effectively with each other, passionately sharing viewpoints, negotiating trade-offs, and working through the inevitable conflicts. People need to feel heard. This is not the same thing, however, as needing to agree with the decisions all the time.

Discuss Decision-making Models with Your Team

There's more than one way to make a decision. Here's a list of options that anyone can understand. In fact, I taught my Girl Scout troop of 11- and 12-year-olds these processes. If they can make them work, so can you!

Executive Decision. Sometimes because of non-negotiable concerns (e.g., safety or politics) or unavoidable circumstances or timing, the leaders will make an executive decision, with or without consulting the group.

Executive Delegation. Sometimes the leader will delegate the decision to the person they feel is best equipped to make it. That person will decide, with or without consulting other group members.

Consensus. Consensus means that everyone accepts and supports the decision, even if it was not their first choice. Discuss the options, with everyone having a say. As you narrow your options, ask everyone to state their number on this scale:

1. Yes! I love this option!
2. Yes. This option is acceptable to me.
3. OK. I can live with this option.
4. I really don't like this option, but I will not block it.
5. I do not agree with this option at all and will block this choice.

If everyone is a 1, 2, or 3, you have a decision. If you have 4s and 5s, continue discussing and negotiating to address concerns. You can move forward as long as there are no 5s.

Majority Rules. Discuss the options, with everyone having a say. Take a vote – one person, one vote. The option with most votes wins.

Last Option Standing. Discuss the options, with everyone having a say. Take a vote on the option you like LEAST. Remove that one, and vote again on the option you like least, until only one remains. That's the winner. This is sometimes the best approach when there are no good options and you are interested in finding the "least worst" approach.

Dot Voting. Discuss the options, with everyone having a say. Be sure that the choices are very different so you don't end up splitting votes between similar options. Everyone is given three or five dots (or votes) to distribute however they like. The option with most votes wins. This method allows those who feel strongly to weight their votes while still giving everyone an equal say.

If the need for consensus and certainty are slowing down your work, you might think more collaboration will only make that worse. But that's not true. Instead you need to step back and review your collaboration processes and how decisions are made.

CHAPTER 9

Openly Recognize Conflicts and Actively Resolve Them

Conflicts about nonprofit communication strategies and implementation are inevitable. I'd say half of the mentoring conversations I have with communications directors are about an office conflict.

Caroline C. Packard, author of an article entitled *Resolving Conflicts in Nonprofit Organizations* and a lecture on *Mediation and Conflict Resolution in Nonprofits*, says that conflict is unavoidable in the nonprofit sector and that some aspects of nonprofit culture can contribute to the conflicts.

For example, people care deeply about the work. Diversity of cultures and experiences, societal change, big dreams, and making something out of nothing are all considered positive values in the sector. But these same elements can be major sources of conflict internally, especially when the lines of authority are blurry. Nonprofit leaders usually fancy themselves as inclusive, but often fail to actively manage or train staff how to be collaborative, which results in indecisiveness and unresolved conflicts.

In the absence of putting in the time and effort to resolve conflicts, we often just go our own separate ways, doing what serves our own priorities. Frankly, in many situations, that's what I recommend communications directors do! You'll often hear me recommend that if you can't get leadership to decide, then you should go ahead and make the decision yourself, assuming it falls within the purview of your work.

But in many cases, that's just not practical nor will it get you to the best outcomes. When communications decisions affect multiple staff members, multiple organizational goals or the larger organizational brand, it's essential that you try to have these conversations, even if you don't reach consensus. It simply doesn't work for executives, program staff, fundraising staff, and communications staff to pursue different and often conflicting communications strategies.

Don't be afraid of conflict or assume that it only refers to big, horrible fights. Packard defines conflict as "uncomfortable differences that make it difficult to work effectively together and that people have tried unsuccessfully to resolve, leaving them feeling stuck and frustrated." We've all felt stuck and frustrated, maybe even daily, which means we've all dealt with the effects of unresolved conflicts.

Conflict resolution helps people go from being "frustrated, stuck, exhausted, wary, and skeptical" to being "at ease about engaging the issues, clearer about their own and other's needs, more confident that a solution may be found, and better able to discover mutually agreeable, workable, realistic solutions," says Packard.

In her lecture, Packard says you'll often find conflict in these seven situations:

- How work is allocated or scheduled.
- How information is shared and with whom.
- How decisions are made and by whom.
- How meetings are run.
- How people behave toward each other.
- Whether and how people get work done.
- Whether and how to resolve people's complaints.

What do these conflicts look like in practice for nonprofit communicators? Here are some common examples.

"My desk is a dumping ground for everyone's brilliant ideas. They all think they are communications experts."

If you try hard enough, practically anything can be labeled "communications." With so much variety in the work, others have ample opportunity to define your job in their own ways. They will make suggestions for what you should be doing, or even outright demand it, often without any strategic consideration attached.

"They expect me to read their minds."

Managers don't include communications staff in meetings where key details are discussed and decisions are made, so communications staff don't have the context they need to create effective messaging, nor the time needed for high-quality creative work.

"We fight constantly about the best images to use in our communications."

The communications or program staff want to talk about upbeat outcomes and use smiling children in the photos. The fundraisers want to talk about the desperate needs that donors can help address and use unhappy children in the photos.

"The program team got really snarky about how I dumbed down the description of their work by saying it was now totally inaccurate.

But there's no way people outside these walls will understand all of their wonky jargon."

The program staff and managers often insist on speaking their expert "insider" language when communications and fundraising staff want to talk more simply and plainly to those outside the organization who don't need the same level of detail and won't understand the nuances in the jargon.

I bet you can come up with an example of each of these within your own organization!

Guiding Yourself and Coworkers Through Conflict Resolution

After coaching many communications directors about office conflicts and learning about executive conflict resolution from Andrew Neitlich, author of the *Coach Master Toolkit*, I recommend this five-step process to resolve conflicts in your office. Share this process with participants ahead of time, so they understand the structure you are using.

STEP 1: Get acknowledgement that a problem exists, the costs associated with it, and the benefits of resolving it.

Think through the following questions yourself, and talk through them together, as appropriate.

What becomes possible for the organization if the conflict is resolved? What becomes possible for staff individually? A compelling picture of what's possible once the conflict is resolved (and the consequences and missed opportunities if it isn't) can be a huge motivator to work through the process.

What are the costs to the organization if this conflict is not resolved? What are the costs to individuals? What's the best you can both expect if you don't resolve this conflict? What's the worst you can expect if you don't resolve it?

Also consider **how much responsibility you are willing to take** for resolving the conflict. Keep in mind intangibles like your pride, being right, looking good, feeling in control, etc. may be at play. Are you willing to apologize or to acknowledge past mistakes if those are standing in the way of good conversations about the future? Some of this may be difficult to voice, but do your best to trust each other through this process.

STEP 2: Listen to each other and be specific.

Share your respective goals with each other. Ask each other a lot of questions. What are you each trying to accomplish? Where do these goals intersect and where do they diverge? What needs are not being met?

What's most important to each of you?

Are there any new facts or perspectives that the other person may not be aware of?

The devil is in the details. Unfortunately, we often carry conclusions from one interaction with a person over to other conflicts, even if the details have changed. Get really clear with each other about where the problems are by being as specific as possible about the particular situation in front of you.

Acknowledge the other's concerns. Don't jump to correcting the person, making your case, or shifting the conversation to a different topic. Your job is to listen for understanding. You don't have to agree with what you are hearing, but you do need to respectfully convey that you understand it and accept it as legitimate in the eyes of the other person.

STEP 3: Clarify your criteria for a workable solution and what flexibility you can offer.

What are you willing to give up to resolve the conflict? What can you offer in exchange for what you need? Where can you be flexible? What can be changed under the right circumstances?

Where are you inflexible? What can't be changed under any circumstances?

How does the other person's approach affect your goals?

STEP 4: Reframe the conflict into specific desired outcomes.

What is it that you really need from each other? After going through Steps 1-3, the answer to this question will likely change.

With your newfound knowledge of each other's situations and concerns, is there a way to reframe the conversation?

Is there a way to integrate the goals so they are both met at once? Or is there a way to keep the work towards one goal from getting in the way of the other goal?

If you reach an impasse, pause and try one of these approaches:

- Take turns restating each other's positions to each other. This allows additional clarifications that can break an impasse.
- Break the problem into smaller chunks. It may be easier to tackle that way.
- Shift gears from process to emotions, or the reverse. If you are stuck on process, set it aside for the moment and check in with how everyone is feeling about the conflict and the

path toward resolution. If the conversation is too emotional, shift toward a more analytical discussion of the process you are working through.

- Restate and validate the areas of agreement. Recenter the conversation on the positive outcomes of the conversation and build from those.

STEP 5: Identify and test solutions, then choose a course of action.

Discuss different options for resolving the conflict. Do not decide now. You are generating alternatives and exploring them.

Test the options with questions like:

- Does this seem fair? Is it a balanced approach?
- Is it realistic? Is it possible to follow through without generating a lot of additional conflict?
- Do you need to get buy-in from others, and how likely is that?

When you are ready, commit to a course of action. Be explicit about what happens next.

Who needs to be informed about this decision? Who will do what tasks and by when?

What contingencies can you put in place to address any lingering fears or potential negative outcomes?

When will you check in with each other to ensure the plan is working and to make any needed adjustments?

Conflict is a natural and healthy part of collaboration. Don't avoid it, or ask everyone to get along nicely as a substitute. Instead, help your coworkers learn how to openly discuss and resolve their conflicts.

PART 3

Be More Agile

A is for Agile. It's the WHEN and WHERE of your communications work.

In the nonprofit sector, change is constant. The same is true for communications and marketing. It's constantly evolving. Good communications work requires you to be nimble and constantly adapting the pace; sometimes slowing down your work, other times speeding it up. To be successful, it's helpful to be good on your feet and to know how and when to bend so that you don't break.

When You Are Agile . . .	When You Aren't Agile . . .
You've established excellent working relationships that help you stay current and responsive.	Your communications are boring and stale because they don't reflect what is really happening today, on the ground, now.
Your management team doesn't feel the need to look over your shoulder because they trust your judgement.	You are locked into rigid communications plans and processes with many layers of review.
You can respond quickly and appropriately to both challenges and opportunities.	You miss great opportunities left and right because you are too slow to capitalize on them.
You take risks and experiment openly, because you understand that's the fastest way to learn.	You hunker down and play it safe.
You think about the future, anticipating how possible changes could affect your nonprofit's communications strategy.	You do what you've always done, and focus more on the past than the present or future.

Why Being Agile is So Important

Being agile means thinking, deciding, and acting quickly and skillfully. But it's more than that. What allows that to happen within organizations is trust. If you don't have the trust of your coworkers and management, you'll be immobilized by layers of review, delays, and endless second-guessing.

Based on the research in Nonprofit Marketing Guide's 2016 and 2017 *Nonprofit Communications Trends Reports*, we know that the quality of the relationship between the communications staff and the executive director has a direct impact on agility, and therefore on communications effectiveness.

We asked communications directors to rate the relationship with their executive directors as exceptional, functional, or difficult. More than half of the most effective communications teams (52%) reported exceptional relationships with their executive directors, with just 4% calling the management relationship difficult.

Conversely, only 17% of ineffective teams report an exceptional relationship between their communications staff and executive directors, with 30% saying it's difficult.

This research shows that a merely functional relationship isn't enough. To get the best results, you need to strive for an exceptional working relationship between the executive director and communications staff.

Keep in mind that the quest for agility doesn't mean living in a constant reactionary state of mind. You still need strategies and plans. It's your ability to adjust those plans that makes you agile, not the ability to work without them.

In each of the seven chapters in this section, you'll explore proven ways for communications staff to build relationships and work habits that lead to agility. Once you have the trust of others, you can more easily build agility into your own planning and day-to-day management of your communications work.

CHAPTER 10

Take Responsibility for Improving Internal Relationships

Leaders and followers have different but equally important skills and roles in any partnership. Regardless of job titles, sometimes we are leaders and sometimes we are followers, depending on the circumstances. You need to know when you are leading and when you are following, and use the right skills at that time.

In their book, *Leadership is Half the Story: A Fresh Look at Followership, Leadership, and Collaboration*, Marc Hurwitz and Samantha Hurwitz say that leaders don't leave their staffs with blank slates. Leadership is about setting the goals and the defining the frame in which the work will be done to achieve those goals. Hurwitz describes it much like a picture frame: leaders provide the frame with some guidelines on what should go inside, but followers use their own talents to create the artwork appropriate for that frame.

Part of framing for leaders is also defining success and building optimum conditions. It's up to them to clarify their vision and expectations. They must also communicate constraints or limitations while gathering resources and eliminating barriers, say the authors.

In contrast, followership is about pursuing the leader's goals and creating within that given frame, write the authors. Followers must get informed and take initiative. They should look for ways to add value and to expand ideas and bring new ones forward. They should help their leaders make good decisions and then support those decisions.

If leadership is not clear, it's up to the follower to get clarification. If the frame is not articulated in a way that you can understand, you need to ask questions. If the frame is not producing optimal results, you need to provide feedback. Followers should think and work *outside* the box, but *inside* the frame, say the Hurwitzs.

Think about some of your work situations where you are the leader. Are you providing a solid frame in which others can follow?

When you are the follower, are you doing all you can within that frame to help the team be successful?

In *Leadership is Half the Story*, the authors say relationship building and "interpersonal agility" are essential workplace competencies today. "Managing up" and understanding how to best collaborate with your managers is certainly an important skill for a communications director. The same is true with "managing across" to coworkers throughout your organization.

Managing these relationships is your responsibility and is essential to your success as a communications director. As the first communications staffer at the Kentucky Equal Justice Center, in Lexington, Kentucky, Marcie Timmerman knew she would need to establish a rapport with each staff person. "I can't do anything effectively without information," says Marcie. Even though staff are spread out across the state, Marcie meets with a staff member each month to touch base about her communications work. "That way, I get to see them in action, and take photos, as well as maintain a rapport," says Marcie. "The rapport is the most crucial part of making my life as a communicator easier. They think of me and my needs and my work because they genuinely know and like me." In addition, she checks in with staff regularly via email and phone calls. "This reminds them that our organization has a story to tell, and they've hired me to tell it," says Marcie.

If you need some help with relationship building and building rapport, consider the questions below. The goal of these questions is to help bring some clarity to how you should manage your workplace relationships or to alert you to some potential blind spots you should think about.

How does your manager or coworker define success in their role?

What are their most important performance goals and initiatives?

How does your manager or coworker define personal success? What are their specific personal goals and aspirations?

What is your manager's or coworker's communication style? What about their productivity styles (e.g. how do they prefer to work)?

What is your manager's or coworker's tolerance for risk and change?

What are two-three attitudes or behaviors from employees/ colleagues that are sure to upset your manager or coworker?

What are up to five things you must do well to meet your manager's or coworker's expectations?

If you can't answer the questions, try one or more of these ideas:

- Email some of these questions to your managers or coworkers, expressing that you'd like to better understand the work of your organization from their perspectives, and how you can best help them.
- Schedule a time to talk to each other about these questions. Lunch?
- Weave a question or two into ongoing conversations you are already having about the work in a more casual way.

Try to understand your role as a leader or follower in your various working relationships and situations and be agile as you shift back and forth between the two. Taking responsibility for building rapport with others will greatly improve your abilities in both roles.

CHAPTER 11

Build Trust in Your Competence

D o you recognize any of these scenarios?

- Your boss is a perfectionist which makes them nitpicky and hypercritical of your work because they believe it reflects poorly on them if it is not just so.
- Even though your boss knows you can do the work, they still think they can do it better, and therefore won't delegate it to you. But because they are so busy, they never actually do the work.
- Your boss says social media is your job, but wants to approve the wording of most posts in advance. Their tweaks seem minor to you, but major to them.

In all of these cases, your competence is being questioned.

This questioning can take many forms: passive aggressiveness, second guessing, failure to assign responsibilities, and more. When your competence is trusted, you are more likely to be given more latitude and control over your work.

Linda A. Hill and Kent Lineback, co-authors of *Being the Boss: The 3 Imperatives for Becoming a Great Leader*, break down competence into three elements: technical knowledge, operational knowledge, and political knowledge. While their advice is directed at managers working with staff, it works in reverse too. You can use their frameworks to build trust with your managers as well as your coworkers.

Hill and Lineback say that *technical knowledge* is what you need to know about the substance of your work. This applies to both the mission of your organization and to your work as a communications professional.

On the mission side, you don't need the same level of expertise as your program staff. But you do need to have a good grasp on the mission of your organization and its programs and services. That means being able to accurately describe the programs. You should understand key terminology and use it correctly in your communications.

On the communications side, however, you are expected to be the expert. For example, you should know how to manage an editorial calendar, how to create compelling content, and how to use communications technology like your email service provider and social media platforms.

Operational knowledge, say Hill and Lineback, is the practical knowledge of how the work gets done within your organization. It's the difference between knowing something in theory (technical knowledge) and being able to actually get it done at work.

For communications staff, operational knowledge includes understanding the programmatic life of your organization (see the *Big Picture Communications Timeline* in Chapter 4) and the opportunities and constraints involved in delivering programs and services.

It also includes understanding how to create the most efficient and effective workflows in your organization to get communications content created and published.

Finally, Hill and Lineback talk about *political knowledge* as the ability to exercise influence effectively. This is largely about your ability to understand interpersonal relationships and motivations of others.

Take these steps to build trust in your competence:

- Take control of your own professional development. Figure out what you need to know and find a way to learn it.
- Be prepared to explain yourself. Do so without being defensive.
- Ask good questions. Don't pretend to understand when you don't.
- Don't undermine others or make them look bad. You may not fully understand the politics they are dealing with.
- Involve others in your work. Show them how you do it – carry that editorial calendar around with you!

Building and maintaining trust in your competence is an ongoing need for all communications professionals. If you feel your competence is in question, don't panic or over-react. Instead, explore whether you should focus on shoring up your technical, operational, and/or political knowledge.

CHAPTER 12

Build Trust in Your Intentions

Most of the trust issues I see in nonprofit communications work are best defined as competence issues (see Chapter 11). However, that's not always the case.

Unfortunately, extraordinarily competent people can have very bad intentions. Think of any classic movie villain, and remember how they used their powers for evil, rather than good. Of course, in nonprofit work, we want to assume that people are using their powers for good. But let's face it: human nature is not always so high-minded. Office politics and personal motivations can make us question each other's motives, or intentions.

If your boss or coworkers think that you are only looking out for yourself, are trying to make yourself look good, are indifferent to their needs, or even worse, are out to get them, you have a trust problem. They need to know that you want the organization to succeed and that you want them to succeed, all before they see your desire for personal success. Transparency about your work, why you are making the choices you are, and what you are trying to achieve, is critical.

In *Being the Boss: The 3 Imperatives for Becoming a Great Leader,* Linda A. Hill and Kent Lineback recommend three approaches.

First, they say to talk explicitly about your intentions. Explain yourself.

Talk clearly about your communications goals and what you are trying to achieve with your communications and why. Invite discussion so that you can get more understanding and buy-in. Hold regular editorial meetings and share your editorial calendar. Share progress reports or dashboards with the metrics you use to measure your progress.

Next, Hill and Lineback say to demonstrate integrity, which they define as walking the talk and keeping your word. Say what you mean, and mean what you say.

The biggest danger for communications directors here is in over-committing and over-promising. You need to be honest about your capacity to get the work done in a timely manner. Don't constantly miss deadlines – speak up well in advance.

Finally, Hill and Lineback urge you to be consistent. Your intentions should be the same from day-to-day and person-to-person. Any differences should be explained.

For communications directors, this can be challenging because not all programs, or news about programs, is equal. The people reading your communications will likely favor some of the work you do over other programs. You may need to shower more communications attention onto some programs to achieve your marketing and fundraising goals. That's appropriate and strategic. It simply needs to be explained well, so there's no misunderstanding about "playing favorites."

Don't let your coworkers and managers guess at your intentions. Be clear, specific, and transparent to avoid misunderstanding and assumptions that could endanger their trust in you, limiting your ability to be agile.

CHAPTER 13

Step Up and Lead

Just about every week, I talk to nonprofit communications directors who have limiting beliefs that are holding them back. Limiting beliefs are ideas or assumptions that you have about yourself, your situation, or others that limit your ability to succeed. They hold you back.

But as I learned from Andrew Neitlich, author of the *Coach Master Toolkit*, when I went through my executive coach training, limiting beliefs are just that: beliefs. They are not indisputable facts, and they are often flat-out wrong. In my role as a coach, I help communications directors challenge their limiting beliefs such as:

- I haven't been given permission or authority to make this decision or to do this work.
- I don't have enough information or experience.
- Saying "no" to a manager or coworker will make me a bad employee, or they just won't like me.
- The risk of trying something is too high.
- I need to be perfect.
- If I mess up, our clients will suffer a grievous harm.

- I am dispensable, so I must lay low and play it safe.
- I don't have enough time or resources or support to do a good job.

While each of these beliefs could be true in theory—and they can certainly feel true when you've had a particularly long and frustrating day—the reality is that they rarely are.

What's more often the case is that people within your organization are hoping you'll put your fears aside and step up, even if they never say that out loud.

If strategic communications leadership is lacking right now, stop waiting for your executive director or board to do something. You could be waiting forever. In many cases, they don't know what to do, or don't really want to do it, or don't want to invest in being good at it.

But they don't admit any of that, or even acknowledge it. They are often confused or lost or even totally clueless. And same goes for your coworkers. They are busy trying to be experts on their own jobs.

It's time for you to step up and lead, from right where you are. After all, they hired YOU.

Sometimes limiting beliefs develop because of organizational cultures that make you doubt or question yourself.

If everything feels last minute and staff are constantly dropping things in your lap after the deadlines, that's a cultural problem that will take time and leadership to change. Odds are that leadership will need to come from—you guessed it—you. If you are constantly sucking it up and doing things at the last minute because of poor planning on the part of your coworkers, you are reinforcing their bad behavior.

It's not unreasonable for staff to expect real strategy, real leadership, and a supportive office culture. If you aren't getting that, make your own choice to be bold and ask for it. And if that doesn't work, be even bolder and make those hard choices yourself.

Quit waiting for someone else to fix it. "Just do it" and "be the change you seek."

CHAPTER 14

Make Better Decisions Faster

On more than a few occasions, I've told friends and family that the gift I most want on my birthday or Mother's Day is to NOT be asked to make a decision. I make what feels like a million decisions in managing work and family, and it's exhausting. This respite from my "decision fatigue" is a real gift.

Your decision-making ability is like a muscle – when you use it too much, you get tired and your performance wanes. That's when decision fatigue sets in. The fatigue compounds when you have lots of options to choose from every time you are presented with a decision to make. And you get to the point where You. Just. Can't. Even.

Think about the enticing items at the grocery store counter: candy bars and gossip magazines that you would normally avoid. But after you've just made a hundred decisions up and down the aisles (just how many varieties of granola bars and cereal do Americans really need?), you are weakened and pick up the Snickers and the *Us Weekly* as you stand there waiting your turn.

This happens all the time in nonprofit marketing and fundraising too.

There are so many different approaches, so many different "best practices" and not enough time or resources to work through them all. You make hundreds of little decisions about your communications work every single day (which shade of green? how big should the logo be? do we include that link in that post? should this be an email or a Facebook post? and on and on). You are pulled in lots of different directions. You can get overwhelmed and caught in a few less-than-ideal scenarios:

- You avoid the decision, and try to do it all, resulting in a mediocre job at best.
- You avoid the decision, and keep doing what you've always done, missing opportunities for real growth.
- You make bad decisions in haste.

How can you structure the way you approach your work to minimize the amount of decision fatigue?

Here are four strategies to make nonprofit communications decision making less exhausting.

Make the Big Decisions Early

We've all been there. You finally get the communications strategy on the agenda for the board meeting, or the staff retreat, but it's at the end. Your time not only gets cut in half because other sections ran over, but everyone is tired and ready to get out of there, so they blow through it. It's not that they don't care about your communications strategy; it's that they are worn out by decision fatigue.

If you have an important decision, best to make it in the morning, or toward the beginning of the meeting agenda. Save the less important stuff for the end of the day or later in the agenda.

Can't get on the agenda early? The next best position is right after a nice long break, like lunch. People are more likely to be temporarily re-energized then.

Delegate Decisions that Really Aren't That Critical

Know what's really important, and what really doesn't matter so much. Let other people make some of those decisions. Or automate them using various productivity programs that do things like sort your inbox for you. FOMO—fear of missing out—is a potential problem here. Acknowledge the trade-off (keeping more of your decision-making energy instead of having your hands in everything) and move on.

Limit Analysis to Three Options at a Time

When you do need to make a decision with lots of options, chunk it. Don't try to fully analyze 10 different approaches, or even five, at once. Make your first decision the one that narrows your options down to three. Explore those. If you decide that none of those three works, then ditch them all, and look at three more.

Create Routines and Habits So You Can Make Fewer Decisions

Create more "simple rules" and routines to automate decision making. This is why you often see CEOs wearing the same outfits and eating the same thing for breakfast and lunch. It's one less decision they have to make about something that really doesn't matter that much to them.

In their book, *Simple Rules: How to Thrive in a Complex World*, Donald Sull and Kathleen M. Eisenhardt define simple rules as "shortcut strategies that save time and effort by focusing our attention and simplifying the way we process information." They help us simplify complex systems and decisions, so that we can move more quickly through our daily lives at work and home.

Sull and Eisenhardt say that the advice to "never go on a second date with someone who only talks about themselves" is a simple rule. Triage procedures used in emergency rooms and on battlefields based on pulse and respiration are simple rules. Nonprofit marketing and fundraising have simple rules too.

If you have a hard time making marketing and fundraising decisions at your nonprofit, or get bogged down in the endless communications choices, creating some simple rules can help. Sull and Eisenhardt offer three different kinds of rules to provide frameworks for making better decisions: Boundary Rules, Prioritizing Rules, and Stopping Rules.

Boundary Rules are the "in or out" or "yes or no" or "always or never" rules. Instead of weighing every conceivable factor, boundary rules hone in on the essential elements and are a great way to translate broad policies into practical guidelines on what to do.

Nonprofit social media policies are based on boundary rules. When do you delete a comment from your Facebook page, for example? Many nonprofits say they will delete posts that contain profanity, spam, personal attacks, promotion of illegal activities, and so forth. Those are clearly stated boundaries that are easily enforced.

Here's another Boundary Rule I use and recommend to communications directors all the time: never spend time creating a piece of content unless you can use it in three different ways. Building content and repurposing into your workflow is essential to both your marketing success and your productivity. This rule helps you focus on content you can use in many different ways over content that is too niche.

Prioritizing Rules help you rank alternatives. Think of them as built-in criteria for decision-making. Once the choices meet the criteria of your Boundary Rules, what next? That's where Prioritizing Rules can help.

Every time your to-do list is way too long (in other words, every day), you use Prioritizing Rules to make choices about what gets done that day. Unfortunately, many times these rules are subconscious and emotionally easy to enforce, even if they don't make sense strategically. Here's one: the squeaky wheel (or loudest or highest-ranking staff member) gets the grease, even if a different, quieter part (or person or project) really needs the attention for the whole machine to reach peak performance.

Spend some time thinking about the Prioritizing Rules you actually use, versus what they should be.

Think about your goals and primary target audiences. What rules can you create so that the "important" comes before the "urgent" as much as possible?

For example, here are some productivity-related Prioritizing Rules:

- Only check your email a few times a day, or at certain times of day, so that you can focus on important work.

- Use time-blocking in your calendar, so you avoid multi-tasking and focus your attention on only one project at a time.
- Establish "office hours" where you welcome drop-in conversations, as well as "closed door" time where you can work uninterrupted.

Stopping Rules do just that – they tell you when to stop looking at alternatives, or when to stop doing certain kinds of work and to change course.

The three questions in my "Quick and Dirty" Marketing Plan are a great example of Stopping Rules:

- Who are we speaking to?
- What's our message to them?
- How do we deliver that message to those people?

If you can't answer those three questions, I say you shouldn't move forward with a communications idea. You stop the work until you can answer all three.

Limiting the number of decisions you have to make each day, and using simple rules to make them, will improve your agility in managing your communications workload effectively.

CHAPTER 15

Expect the Unexpected

You don't know what's going to happen in the future. But you do know that something you'll have to deal with is going to come up. So you need to accept that reality.

Here are several ways you can stay agile and plan for the unexpected so that it doesn't throw you off your game when it happens.

Follow the Editorial Calendar Rule of Thirds

When building an editorial calendar for the first time, I recommend using the rule of thirds: one-third of your calendar is filled with original or curated content, one-third is filled by repurposing the first third, and you leave the final third open for all of the stuff that comes up. For example, if you usually have three articles in a newsletter, you could plan two with strategic content and leave the third open until closer to publication time.

Develop Standard Workflows
for the Most Likely Communication Problems

All communication directors have their personal nightmare days, and they often include incidents like these:

- Your website got hacked or went down.
- Several people were offended by some of your content and backlash is growing.
- You were caught totally unprepared when a reporter called about breaking news.

All communications directors should work through common scenarios like these. Openly talk about who has the authority to do what. Who gets to make what decisions and who needs to see what? In those gray areas, be clear about what needs to be communicated to whom before a decision can be made, and the expectations for turnaround times.

Take the website going down, for example. Do you just sit there and do nothing, hoping it comes back up on its own? Of course not. Maybe the workflow looks something like this:

1. Confirm it's the website and not just the internet connection or browser.
2. Call the hosting company and ask them to help diagnose and fix the problem.
3. If the hosting company can't bring the site back up immediately, redirect the domain to another site like your Facebook Page until the problem is resolved.

Naturally, you'd want to include phone numbers, account numbers, and whatever else someone would need to actually follow the process.

Outline Plans for More Dramatic, But Less Likely Crisis Scenarios

Do you fear that your whole game plan could be destroyed by some major crisis? You can manage that too, if you are prepared.

At a training I once presented, we played a "challenges/solutions" game inspired by an exercise in *Gamestorming: A Playbook for Innovators, Rulebreakers, and Changemakers*.

I called it "What Could Possibly Go Wrong Next?!?" and presented two basic scenarios: a potential food poisoning at a Meals on Wheels and a United Way executive making an insensitive or politically incorrect statement.

Some tables were asked to brainstorm what could go wrong next. In the meal delivery case, they came up with things like "someone died from the food poisoning" and "a volunteer knew the food was tainted." In the scenario about the gaffe, the challengers came up with things like "this wasn't the first time he was caught on video saying something like that" and "big donors are pulling support."

The other tables were tasked with coming up with a set of tools, responses, etc. that they could use during a crisis – but not yet knowing what the challengers were coming up with.

We then played out the game in front of the larger group, with the challengers playing a card, and the solutions team playing one or two cards in response. The rest of the room then voted on whether the response was enough to address the crisis. In both cases, we said the nonprofits were able to "swim" rather than "sink" – but it was a close call!

I urge you to play a version of the game within your own nonprofit, as it's really the best way to prepare for your own potential crisis.

You can't always control what happens, but you can control your reaction to it. With some imagination and planning, you can respond with agility when things go wrong.

C H A P T E R   1 6

Create Agile Content

Repurposing your content is essential to your success. You don't have enough time to create original content constantly, and your community needs to hear your messages and calls to action in clear and consistent ways over and over anyway. Repurposing content makes sense, and it works!

As you've seen in previous chapters, I like "simple rules" that create reasonable and repeatable workflows. So I created five of them to help guide your repurposing strategy. To make them even easier to remember, they are all "rules of three."

Rule #1: The Editorial Calendar Rule of Thirds

As I've mentioned previously, when you plan your editorial calendar, think about the number of times you'll be communicating in all of your given communications channels within a set amount of time. Plan for about a third of those slots to contain original content. Plan for another third to contain repurposed content (either from that first third or older content). The final third you leave open because you know something will come up that you'll need to add. If it's a slow time, repurpose more content into those slots!

Rule #2: Deconstruct Big Ideas into Three Smaller Chunks

When you come up with great ideas for content, as you are writing, think about how you would break that idea into at least three smaller ideas. For example, let's say you need to do some wrap-up and thank-you messaging after a fundraiser. You might want to do one big post on your blog, but think about it in at least three chunks that you could parse out for other communications channels or smaller articles. Your three chunks might be: (1) How much you raised and what you will do with the money, (2) the photo gallery from the event and (3) some highlights or quotes from people who were there. By thinking ahead of time, even if you are doing longer pieces initially, your repurposing work will be so much easier.

Rule #3: Formats – Long Form, Short Form, Visual Form

Think about three different ways to format your content. When possible, do a long form, a short form, and a visual form. If that's not possible, you can mix and match, or even do three different types of one form (e.g. a post on Facebook, Instagram, and Twitter, all tweaked to perform best in each channel).

Different Ways to Repurpose Content

Long Forms	Short Forms	Visual Forms
• Blog Posts	• Email Teaser Blurbs	• Video
• Website Articles	• Facebook	• Slideshare
• Newsletter Articles	• Twitter	• Stories on
• White Papers	• Instagram	Snapchat,
• E-books	• Photos with	Instagram,
• Presentations	Captions	Facebook
• Medium	• Email	• Infographics
• LinkedIn	Autoresponders	• Or go interactive:
• Guest Posts	• Media Pitches	• Quiz
• Op-Eds	• Invitations	• Worksheet

Rule #4: Time Zones – Now, Soon, Later

In many cases, the time periods in which we repurpose content are too short. Instead of thinking about just this week or next week, how could you plan to repurpose content you are writing this week for a month from now? A quarter from now? Next year?

Think about ways to repurpose now, soon, and later. But also consider repurposing within a campaign, for example. How can you reuse content at the beginning, middle, and end of a campaign? What would it look like if you considered how you would use today's content again later this month, next quarter, and next year? Can you make changes to the way you write now that will facilitate that repurposing later?

Rule #5: Everything in at Least Three Channels

This is my last rule in the list, but it was the first repurposing rule I developed for myself. Never create anything unless you know how you are going to use it in at least three different communications channels. If it is so niche or specialized that it's only good for use in one communications channel, you aren't thinking creatively enough, or it's not worth your time to create.

Repurposing content is one of the skills that sets communications pros apart from the novices. Build content agility into your work habits and the results will pay off for years to come.

PART 4

Be More Logical

L is for Logical – It's the WHAT and WHY of your communications work.

Many people mistakenly believe that good marketing is all about the creative: the right words, the perfect images. While those are important, they don't matter without a logical strategy as their foundation. Communications work, even in its most creative forms, should always be clear in purpose and backed by reason. If your nonprofit marketing work isn't grounded in something that makes sense organizationally, you will encounter many problems.

When You Are Logical...	When You Aren't Logical...
Your communications goals are well integrated into how the nonprofit gets its mission work done.	Decision making will be painfully slow, because there is no logical basis for how to decide.
You use reasonable and well-understood criteria to decide what communications work gets done and why.	You are at the mercy of others' instincts (no matter how poorly informed), or ideas that sound good, but aren't likely to succeed given your circumstances.
Program staff not only respect and value the expertise within the communications team, but understand the time required to do good work.	You will be expected to do it all, trying to please everyone all the time, with a to-do list a mile long.
You'll see clear differences between *urgent, important,* and *urgent and important* items on your to-do list.	You can't prioritize your work, and urgent will constantly overtake the important.
Investments in communications staff and budgets come more easily.	Communications staff and their work will be marginalized because the value isn't clear.

Why Being Logical is So Important

It's not unusual for a communications department to be staffed last and cut first. Why? Because the logical need for professional communications at the organization is not clearly understood or articulated.

When the communications work is understood and valued, a different logic failure can set in: Everything is important and everything is a priority. It's just not true, but it can feel like it without a logical basis for deciding what comes first, second, and third on the priorities list.

Being logical is about reexamining the reasons behind the communications work you are creating. It's about connecting the dots between the communications work product and the larger marketing, fundraising and/or programmatic goals it is meant to help the organization achieve.

In each of the five chapters in this section, you'll explore proven ways for communications staff to be more logical, starting with being more strategic and focused, followed by doing what makes the most sense.

CHAPTER 17

Limit and Integrate Your Communications Goals

O ne day, a nonprofit communications director showed me her brand-new marketing strategy. The organization's leaders, the executive director and a committee of board members, had commissioned the strategy from a consultant. After several months of work, the strategy was delivered to staff to implement.

But the document I saw contained very little leadership or strategy: instead, it was everything and the kitchen sink. The goals were vague. It included nearly every conceivable target group (including the dreaded "general public"), rather poorly aligned with a dozen communications channels. The sections on messaging were clearly written by a Buzzword Bingo champion.

Is This What a Good Strategy Looks Like?

The leaders and the consultant were both apparently very happy with their strategy. But the communications director was confused. She couldn't tell what her goals were or which tactics were most important. She couldn't see how this was supposed to direct her own choices about what she should do at work this week, this month, or even this year. She couldn't see how this strategy would produce results any different from what they were getting now.

She had lots of questions for me: Was this a good strategy? Or was she right in thinking that it really didn't make sense? Or was it her? Was she misunderstanding the vision and direction embedded in the document? Was her own frustration about not being included as the strategy was developed clouding her judgement about the quality of the consultant's work?

I assured her (in my typical blunt way) that the so-called strategy was a load of crap. I commended her for pushing back and asking hard questions of her leaders and the consultant. I encouraged her to continue to challenge the lack of strategy and leadership on display, albeit in a more diplomatic way than using my description.

Anyone with a bit of knowledge or experience can brainstorm a bunch of ideas and put them into tables, throw in some bold here and there, and label it a strategy. And charge thousands for it. But that doesn't make it so.

The process of developing a real strategy includes looking at all the possible things you could do to achieve your goals, which themselves must be limited, clear, and specific. But it doesn't stop there! It winnows those options down to the right combination that is most likely to produce the best results – to the things you will do, backed up with adequate staffing and budgets. It prioritizes, which means saying Item #1 is more important than Item #2, and those are both more important than Item #3.

As Harvard professor and leading expert on competitive strategy Michael Porter says, "Strategy 101 is about choices: you can't be all things to all people. Strategy is about making choices, trade-offs; it's about deliberately choosing to be different."

So who makes those hard choices in the strategy? A good consultant can certainly frame them and queue them up, but the organization's leaders need to actually make those decisions. Failing to choose, failing to prioritize, and failing to say "yes" to some, but more importantly "no" to most are failures of leadership. It's hard—really hard!—to say no to good ideas, but that's what's required to pursue the great ideas. That's leadership.

Pick Goals That Make Sense

Marketing and communications should be viewed as an integral part of your programmatic and fundraising success, which means that there should be some shared or overlapping goals. Everyone else in the organization needs to understand why marketing is essential, and the best way to do that is to link your goals to theirs.

At Nonprofit Marketing Guide, we've learned that nonprofit communications teams are most likely to work on a subset of these 12 goals. Keep in mind that the most effective teams will choose just a few of the goals—not all of them!

Leadership and strategy require selectively choosing from this list.

Community Engagement and Education Goals

- Engaging our community to keep people inspired by, and active in, our work.

- Raising awareness of our issues to educate people on our cause.
- Advocating on our issues to change hearts and minds.

Brand and Leadership Goals

- Brand building and reputation management for the organization.
- Positioning our staff as thought leaders or experts.
- Communicating internally with our staff or board.

Program Recruitment Goals

- Recruiting and engaging participants to use our programs or services.
- Building our membership by recruiting and serving members of our organization.
- Recruiting and engaging volunteers to help deliver our programs and services.

Fundraising Goals

- Supporting fundraising from individuals making small to medium gifts.
- Supporting major donor fundraising.
- Supporting event fundraising (galas, walks, etc.).

Now, which make the most sense for your organization?

While the mission of the organization has little influence on tactical best practices, like which communications channels you use most, it does greatly influence which communications goals are likely to be high priorities.

Overall, across the nonprofit sector, these are the top five communications goals, according to the *Nonprofit Communications Trends Reports*:

- Engaging our community to keep people inspired by, and active in, our work.
- Brand building and reputation management for the organization.
- Raising awareness of our issues to educate people on our cause.
- Supporting major donor fundraising.
- Communicating internally with our staff and board.

But here's how these goals rank as the most important and least important by mission, according to Nonprofit Marketing Guide's *2017 Nonprofit Communications Trends Report*:

Mission	Highest Priority Communications Goals	Lowest Priority Communications Goals
Human Services, Housing, Food, and Jobs	Engaging our community, brand and reputation management, raising awareness of issues	Building our membership, recruiting and engaging volunteers, recruiting and engaging participants
Education	Brand and reputation management, engaging our community, recruiting and engaging participants	Recruiting and serving members, recruiting and engaging volunteers, advocating on issues
Health, Disease, and Medical Research	Brand and reputation management, engaging our community, raising awareness of issues	Recruiting and engaging volunteers, building our membership, recruiting and engaging participants
Environment and Animals	Engaging our community, raising awareness of issues, raising small-medium gifts from individuals	Recruiting and engaging participants, recruiting and engaging volunteers, building our membership
Arts, Culture, and Humanities	Recruiting and engaging participants, engaging our community, brand and reputation management	Recruiting and engaging volunteers, thought leadership, advocating on issues

Association, Membership, and Mutual Benefit	Building our membership, recruiting and engaging participants, brand and reputation management	Recruiting and engaging volunteers, raising small-medium gifts from individuals, major donor fundraising
Religion	Engaging our community, recruiting and engaging participants, raising small-medium gifts from individuals	Supporting fundraising events, recruiting and engaging volunteers, thought leadership
Philanthropy and Grantmaking	Brand and reputation management, major donor fundraising, internal communications	Recruiting or engaging volunteers, building our membership, supporting fundraising events
International	Brand and reputation management, engaging our community, raising small-medium gifts from individuals	Building our membership, recruiting and engaging volunteers, recruiting and engaging participants
Other Public Benefit Research and Advocacy	Engaging our community, raising awareness of issues, advocating on issues	Recruiting and engaging volunteers, building our membership, supporting fundraising events

Your communications team can't function as an island; your goals can't be isolated either. Limiting and integrating your communications goals with other organizational goals will quickly help you establish the logic behind your communications choices.

CHAPTER 18

Keep Up with Shifting Priorities

Do you have a hard time keeping up with the shifting priorities at your organization?

Don't worry – you aren't alone. It's a common predicament for communications staff. Your executive director or management team may be too busy wrestling with the shifts themselves to think through the impact on your communications strategy and editorial calendar.

But keeping up with those shifts and understanding the impact on your short-term and long-term goals is an important part of your work. Here are a few approaches that can help.

Help Staff Visualize Shifting Priorities and the Impacts on Communications

Sometimes it's hard to understand the impact on your communications plans without a visual aid. "We have a giant white board on the wall that is split into categories: this week, next week, this month, future, and idea parking lot," says Megan Bourque-Stith, director of communications at the Ohio Association of Community Health Centers in Columbus, Ohio. The staff uses sticky notes color coded by communications channel to collect task and ideas.

"We meet once a week and reorganize the board, prioritizing, assigning who is going to do what, and brainstorming. Anything that is done goes in a basket so we can see how much we have accomplished. It works really well for us," says Megan.

It's also a big help in explaining the workload of the communications team to others. "They can see all of the things we have on our plate, which is helpful when explaining why we can't send their email three times this week," says Megan. "It has also streamlined our small department as everyone knows what they are supposed to be doing, and we hash out any issues at our weekly meeting."

Ask Leadership to Re-Slice the Priority Pie

Here's another way to get guidance: ask your executive director or coworkers to slice up a pie.

Bring a sheet of paper with a big circle on it into a meeting. Ask the person to take their pen and slice up the pie for you. How they slice it indicates how they feel about the relative importance of each slice – and that's the start of a strategic conversation about priorities.

Let's look at how this could work.

Are you supposed to reach "everyone" with your communications? If that's the case, you can probably rattle off 5-10 segments, like current donors, prospective donors, current clients of your services, prospective clients, volunteers, people who care about your issues, community influencers and leaders, the media, other partner and peer organizations, older people, younger people, and on and on.

Name your pie "Who Should Get the Most Attention in Our Communications" or "Who Our Communications Are Really For" or something like that.

Let them go at it, or you can provide some direction by narrowing down the number of slices they are working with by listing those above the circle. Ask the person to divide the pie among those slices based on how much time or attention they think you should be devoting to those target audiences.

You could also ask a group of people to do this individually and then compare their answers to see the level of consensus you have.

One of four things will most likely happen.

1. **Some of the slices will be bigger than others.** That demonstrates some sense of priority. Now you can discuss the implications of that. How does this match the current reality? What would it take to really make those pie slices bigger in practice? What does it mean to make those other slices smaller?

2. **All the slices will be the same size,** and they may even try to cram in additional slices. This is your opportunity to point out that this approach spreads your attention too thin, making it difficult for you to make any real progress with any one segment. You can do a mediocre job at lots of things, a decent job at a handful of things, or an amazing job at one thing. That's not a value judgement about which to choose – but you do need to choose. Maybe "mediocre on lots of things" is the way you need to go! But make sure that's a conscious choice, not just a default.

3. **They will try to change the assignment** to something else. This might be just fine, if you see how it provides direction

and priorities for your work. If it's distracting from that, try to refocus on the original pie.

4. **They will refuse to slice the pie.** I would take this as a sign that they are delegating decision making to you. Do what you think is right until they tell you that you are wrong, and are willing to discuss it with you.

Here are several different pies you can ask people to slice for you that should lead to strategic conversations about priorities:

- Which goals should get the most attention from communications staff? For example, how do fundraising, community engagement, and brand building compare? See Chapter 17 for information on common goals.
- Which target audiences should get the most attention in our communications?
- Which programs or issues should get the most attention in our communications?
- Which communications channels should get the most time from communications staff?
- Where and how should we spend our communications budget?
- What's the right balance of original content versus repurposed content or content curated from others?

Save these pie slices and revisit them when you sense that priorities are shifting again.

What to Do When Your Visionary Boss Won't Prioritize

As easy as the pie exercise is, some visionary leaders can't even focus on that level of detail. In that case, you might want to try some different approaches.

Discuss What Your Manager Needs from You, and What You Need in Return, for Success. If at all possible, meet with the visionary face to face. Explain that you are inspired by their vision, and as the person charged with implementing it in a concrete way and handling all the messy details, you need their support in setting clear goals and realistic deadlines.

Do Top Priority Checks. You can't stop the idea machine. But you can check in regularly to see where last week's ideas relate to this week's. Always have your Top Three Priorities for the week or month on the tip of your tongue. When assigned another priority, ask the visionary to tell you where it rates compared to your current Top Three. Does it replace something else as a top priority? (Naturally, this works a whole lot better if you have both agreed that "Three Top Priorities" is an appropriate way for you to make choices about where you spend your time and energy.)

Write Up a Quick Summary and Check in Regularly with Drafts. Don't just jump to it and work straight through on a project until completion. Start with a quick email or note—or even a quick verbal check-in—summarizing the project as you understand it and asking for confirmation that you have the concept right. A full creative brief (see Chapter 5) may be called for, but the reality is that the visionary will probably be too busy to review all those details. Then check in regularly with drafts so the visionary has the option to change or cancel the project before you've invested too much time.

Prepare to Repurpose Your Work. You'll put a lot of effort into projects, only to have the plug pulled. If you suspect that outcome, as you work, think about ways that the energy you do put into it could be repurposed into another project later. Keep everything! You never know when you can recycle it! Odds are the visionary won't even recognize it when they see it again.

Practice Benign Neglect. Benign neglect is when you purposely ignore something and as a result, it takes care of itself, usually by falling off the to-do list altogether. If you suspect the visionary will quickly drop this week's hot idea, just sit on it for awhile. Wait to see if it is mentioned again before you invest any time into it.

Shifting priorities are so common in communications work that it's only logical to have a system in place to effectively manage those changes. In the absence of a leader providing communications priorities to you, I believe it's entirely appropriate to lead yourself. Go back to Chapter 13 for some tips.

CHAPTER 19

Learn How to Say "No"

Yyou may not have complete control over your workload, but I bet you have more than you think you do. Or you can get more control with some practice and discipline at saying "no" to new requests for your time and attention.

Saying "no" can be hard, though! And in some cases, or with some people, you might fear some backlash at actually uttering the word out loud.

It's time to get good at saying "no!" without actually saying it that way. Here are eight approaches you can start trying today.

"Let's talk about our goal with this. What are we trying to accomplish?"

People get excited about their great ideas, and this is especially true with communications tactics. If you can redirect the conversation to more strategic questions about goals, target audiences, messaging, etc., you can often help someone see that the idea isn't quite right, or not quite ready, or that you are already doing something else to meet the goal.

"Doing this means I couldn't do _____ this week. Is that a good trade-off?"

Help the person making the request see the trade-off of doing the task. It means you are taking time and attention away from something else. Help them see that, and encourage them to actively discuss with you which task is the priority, and therefore which is not the priority, rather than just adding to the list. Prioritizing is absolutely essential in communications work!

"How about if I _____ instead?"

This is the "no, but" approach. You offer to help in other ways that are less time-consuming or distracting for you, or that you know will be more strategic.

"Can you get me more information?"

Put more of the homework or initial legwork back on the person making the request. If it is that important to them, they will follow through. But often times, they won't. This is a great approach when people make suggestions based on something they saw being done elsewhere, or when the request is simply too vague.

"Let me think about that and get back to you."

Giving yourself a little breathing room is another great tactic. By not saying "yes" or "no" on the spot, you get time to consider the tradeoffs of your answer. Delaying an answer by a few days could also change the context of the request: the person asking may lose their own enthusiasm for it, or the dynamics around the request may change. Whether you actually get back to the person with an answer or just go the "benign neglect" route is your call.

"I'm going to put that on my Good Ideas List."

Everyone should have an "idea parking lot" or "someday" list. Just acknowledging that the idea will not be forgotten, even if it is never actually worked on, may be enough to satisfy someone making the request.

"OK, but not yet."

Sometimes ideas need time to ripen. You can acknowledge that the idea is good, but that the timing is not.

Say nothing at all.

Sometimes silence is the best response. It might encourage the other person to keep talking, and to find another solution, including asking someone else to do it.

If your to-do list is too long and too reactive from saying "Yes" too often, it's logical to practice saying "No."

CHAPTER 20

Follow Best Practices, But Experiment Constantly

You are not the only nonprofit facing marketing challenges. You don't need to start from scratch. Pay attention to what others are doing and start with the best practices associated with whatever it is you are trying to do. We are very blessed in this sector that people share information freely.

But to really make progress, you must be willing to try new things. Sometimes your experiments will work, and sometimes they won't, but you'll always learn something. From that learning, you can logically move on to the next experiment.

Here are 10 relatively simple marketing experiments that I think all communications directors should try.

1. Create a new schedule for repurposing your best content. What if you automatically reshared any evergreen content you create at 3, 6, 9, and 12 months intervals? Or try a different schedule. Will the content work just as well a year after it was created? You might be surprised!

2. Test your email subject lines. Just Google "best email subject lines" and you'll find several lists with great ideas to try.

3. Play with your formulas for social media posts. Does AARP's Rule of One (one photo, one sentence, one link, and one request from readers) work for you? Would another formula you create work better?

4. Will a website pop-up work? Everyone says they hate them, but we know they've worked for many organizations. Think of three calls to action you could add to a pop-up and see what happens.

5. Will curated content work just as well, or better than, original content? Find some good content created by others and share it through your networks, with proper attribution, of course!

6. Play with the length of your content. Make your blog posts or email newsletters shorter or longer. Does it change results or your workload in positive ways?

7. Play with the frequency of your content. Can you post to a certain communications channel more often or less often? Does it have any impact on your results?

8. Change up your work day. Do certain marketing tasks at a different time of day to see if they are easier or you are more productive then.

9. Expand your network by five. Pick five influencers you want to connect with, or five bloggers you want to guest post for, or five events you want to speak at, and work toward those. What did you learn from working with those five that you could apply in the future?

10. Find new marketing peers and exchange ideas. Do coffee, lunch or dinner with someone new in nonprofit marketing or fundraising once a month (or more often!). Document what you learn from your conversations.

It's not logical to expect different results from the same old behavior. Mix it up and play around. You might be pleasantly surprised by the results. Even if you aren't, you are still guaranteed to learn something in the process.

CHAPTER 21

Make Progress on Strategic Goals Every Day

In the everyday hustle and bustle of your work, it's too easy to lose touch with the "why" or the logic behind your work. That's why it's important to track your progress. Doing so helps ground you in the reasoning of your larger strategy and tactical editorial calendar.

The Importance of Taking a Step Forward Each Day, No Matter How Small

What does a really good work day look like for you?

According to research by Teresa Amabile, a professor at Harvard Business School and author of *The Progress Principle: Using Small Wins to Ignite Joy, Engagement, and Creativity at Work* from the Harvard Business School, your best workdays likely include making progress—even if it is just a small win—on work you consider meaningful or important.

Amabile calls this the "progress principle." When she compared her research participants' best and worst days (defined by their mood, specific emotions, and motivation levels), the best days were those where any progress on the work by either the individual or their team took place. If you feel motivated and happy at the end of your workday, odds are good that you made some progress that day.

Nonprofits are built for meaningful work almost by definition. Therefore, we in the sector should have a leg up on good days. But, of course, we all know that's not the way it works. Plenty of people, situations, and events can get in the way of daily progress.

Making a little progress every day is really important to staying motivated and happy in your work. But when you feel like you are getting pulled in a hundred different directions, as many nonprofit communicators are, that can be tough.

Experts recommend that you develop "progress rituals." Here are six I like.

Connect the Dots Between Tactics and Strategy

It's much easier to track your strategic progress if you (1) have a strategy and (2) know what activities support the implementation of that strategy.

Brian Olson, communications manager at Children of the Nations based in Silverdale, Washington, uses both calendars and spreadsheets to keep track of how his work ties back to the nonprofit's strategic plan. "I use a Google Spreadsheet to track everything our department sends out throughout the year, along with the date it's sent, departments affected, cost, revenue generated, and approximate time to produce," says Brian. "All of this comes from a planning document created at the end of the previous year that shows all the major communications initiatives for the coming year, and when we plan to send them out." Naturally, changes do happen throughout the year and the team has to be flexible. "But having a plan and structure really enables us to be collaborative, agile, logical, and methodical," says Brian.

Pick Just One Thing a Day

Your to-do list is way too long, right? I used to try to narrow the list to five things or even three things that I wanted to get done that day. But if I got two out of three done, I felt like I'd failed. So now, I often pick just one important thing. I try to make it truly important, not just urgent. If I can get that one thing done, I will consider the day a success.

That doesn't mean that I don't tackle other things, or quit as soon as the one thing is achieved. But it does mean that I don't beat myself up about the rest of it, and I allow myself to chalk it up as a "good day" if the one important selected to-do gets done.

Actively Manage Your Decision Points

If you bounce from call to email to writing to meeting to interruptions to meeting to Facebook, try this. Immediately upon finishing a task, get very intentional about what you do next.

If you are really bouncing around, you might have 10 or 15 decision points in one day! Stop. Take a few breaths. Think about how much time you have before the next locked-in thing on your schedule. What is the best thing to do next, in the time you have? Get yourself off of autopilot and really think.

Savor each decision point in your day. Plan your decision points in advance. Don't start a new task without consciously deciding it's the right one. Literally say to yourself, "This is a decision point."

Play Your Theme Song

You'll find lots of advice about meditating or taking a walk to refocus your energy during the day. But let's face it: that's just not happening on a hectic day.

But even on the craziest days, you can pop in your ear buds for 30 seconds and play a snippet of one of your favorite songs. We know that music can motivate us and make us feel more successful when exercising, and the same can be true at work. I've found that the songs I have on my exercise playlist are actually pretty good for helping me power through work too.

While I personally don't like to listen to music when I am writing (it's too distracting), I've found that listening to a song or two on my exercise playlist can be just as uplifting when I'm feeling off-track and floundering at work. Personal favorites of mine in 2017 for getting back on track were *The Greatest* by Sia and *Formation* by Beyoncé (#WeSlay).

Start a Progress Journal

Don't just jump into it each day. Give yourself 15 quiet, focused minutes at the start of each day to plan your day. Do this before speaking to anyone or looking at your email or social media. What is most important to you today? What are the Top Three things on your to-do list, in order?

End the day with 15 quiet, focused minutes too. Reflect on how your day went. What did you accomplish? What was frustrating? What do you want to remember about today as you approach tomorrow?

It doesn't have to involve deep thoughts or much time at all. You can even do it on your phone on your commute home. But each day, take a minute or two to jot down three accomplishments from your day, no matter how small. If that sounds like too much, how about a one-sentence journal or recording a 30-second voice memo to yourself? It's not the length or format that matters—it's the reflecting on wins, no matter how small, that counts.

Put it on Your Meeting Agenda

Publicly sharing progress and little wins is another great way to stay on track. We start the beginning of every group call in our Communications Director Mentoring Program with this kind of sharing. You could add it to the agenda of one of your regular meetings. If you know it's on the agenda, you are more likely to think about it ahead of time. It's not only a great way to stay on track, but it also helps participants connect with each other on a personal level.

No matter how you do it, stay connected to the logic of your work every day. It will work for you personally, and for your team as a whole.

PART 5

Be More Methodical

M is for Methodical – It's the HOW of your communications work.

Communications work should follow clear processes and use tools that improve efficiency. If you don't have good methods in place for managing your communications, you'll always feel scattered, rushed, and uncertain. While each person and organization will have their own quirks, there are some basic methods in communications work that are universal. You need systems and regular workflows to add some method to the typical nonprofit communications madness.

When You Are Methodical ...	When You Aren't Methodical ...
You can handle the urgent while never forgetting the important.	Urgent activities always overtake the important ones.
You save so much time on routine work that you have more time to think strategically.	You waste time making up new ways to get the same old work done.
You can delegate tasks and take a vacation with no worries about what's happening back at the office.	You become the only one who can do certain tasks, which creates huge bottlenecks and means you have to work longer and harder, often alone, to get everything done.
Other staff find you easy to work with, because they understand your process and how they can plug into it.	Collaboration with others becomes very time-consuming and incredibly inefficient.
Even when you get distracted or pulled away, you can easily get yourself back on track.	You often fall down the rabbit hole and get lost for hours—if not days—at a time.

Why Being Methodical is So Important

You will always be short on time. You will always be surrounded by distractions. That's why it is so important to be grounded in proven methods that you can always go back to. It's like meditating – it's OK for your mind to wander off, but when it does, you bring the focus back. The same goes with nonprofit marketing.

There is no single job description for a nonprofit communications director, and good nonprofit marketing includes many skills and disciplines (not just writing and design, but psychology and neuroscience, to name a few). While that certainly keeps the job interesting, that kind of work-day diversity can also cause some problems.

In each of the five chapters in this section, you'll explore proven ways for communications staff to be more methodical in planning, creating productive workflows, and managing efficient processes.

CHAPTER 22

Use an Editorial Calendar

No other single tool can shore up your marketing methodology better than an editorial calendar. A good editorial calendar system helps you be CALM in every way: collaborative (because it helps everyone see your communications plan in action and therefore contribute to it); agile (because you build in repurposing and room for the unexpected in the schedule; logical (because you can see how the communications channels and schedules work together toward a goal; and methodical (because creating the calendar is a process others can replicate and follow).

Editorial planning works. Nonprofits with effective communications are three times as likely to use an editorial calendar as those who say their communications are ineffective, according to the 2017 *Nonprofit Communications Trends Report*. Effective communicators are also twice as likely to invest significant time into editorial planning as ineffective ones.

What's Included in an Editorial Calendar

Simply put, an editorial calendar is a tool to manage and schedule the publication of strategic content across multiple channels.

It shows the breadth (which channels) and depth (the frequency) of your communications strategy.

Editorial calendars MUST have all three of these elements:

- Channels – where is the content going out (newsletter, Facebook, etc.)?
- Timing – when is the content going out (usually which day)?
- Message – what is the content about (e.g., topic, call to action)?

You can also add optional elements like:

- Who is responsible.
- Internal deadlines.
- Creative brief or direction.
- What stage the content is in (e.g. idea, draft, review, approved, published).
- Notes or conversations as the content is created.
- Post-publication metrics.

Your editorial calendar will feature original content, curated content, and repurposed content. Remember: we recommend you use the Rule of Thirds to start (see Chapter 15). One third of each: original/curated, repurposed, and unplanned for merging in new topics.

The actual tool used is a personal choice. It can be on paper, on a whiteboard, or online. It can be in a spreadsheet, a calendar, or in a project management tool.

Finding the Right Tool and Process Takes Time

Finding the right tool and workflow process around your editorial calendar can take some time, but it's worth the effort. Consider the process that Sharon Sharp, the marketing and communications associate at SPCA Tampa Bay, went through.

When SPCA Tampa Bay first learned about editorial calendars during a conference presentation I did, they created an Excel document in a shared drive. It included calendar dates down the side and all of their communications channels (social media, direct mail, newsletters, website, e-newsletter and appeals, etc.) across the top.

Departments holding events were asked to add details to the corresponding cell in the spreadsheet, such as times and dates, a blurb about the event, associated registration links, and staff contact information.

Sharon rolled it out with high hopes that were quickly dashed. Program staff didn't use it at all, despite repeated reminders.

After talking to the program staff, Sharon recognized three major problems:

1. The Excel editorial calendar wasn't incorporated into what they were already doing day-to-day. It was another thing added to their to-do list.

2. Without a prompt, staff weren't remembering they needed to communicate information, whether to a person or into the document. The editorial calendar sat passively on the server.

3. Program staff aren't marketers. It was unrealistic to expect program staff to look at a myriad of promotional channels and to ask them to decide how often they should market and where.

The solution? Sharon moved the editorial calendar out of Excel and into Microsoft Outlook. SPCA Tampa Bay uses Outlook for its email and heavily uses the calendar feature for meeting appointments and to reserve resources like rooms and vehicles. "Most staff live by their calendar alerts and view their calendars multiple times a day," says Sharon. "By creating an editorial calendar within Outlook we could check problem #1 off the list: it was a tool everyone was already using."

Sharon starting treating promotional efforts as "appointments to provide content" on the Outlook calendar. She color coded the appointments to communicate information about what marketing channels would be used.

Next she invited relevant staff to each appointment. "This way it shows up on their personal calendar and also creates an automated reminder, which keeps them engaged," says Sharon. There goes problem #2!

When the appointment reminder goes off, the staff person opens the appointment in Outlook and then drops their copy and attaches photos directly into the appointment, where marketing staff can retrieve it when they are ready to draft the content.

Lastly, marketing staff go into the editorial calendar each month and add appointments to map out a suggested marketing plan for each event. As marketing needs change, program staff are encouraged to edit this plan. For instance, they can add an appointment if registrations are low and they want additional promotion. Or if registrations are exceeding capacity, they can delete promotions.

"Using this system, we created a centralized place for information, provided marketing support by creating a skeletal marketing plan for all events, built in the capacity for event staff to update the calendar to reflect any changes in their marketing needs, and created automated prompts to keep them engaged using a tool they were already incorporating into their day," says Sharon. "We have five departments successfully contributing to the calendar!"

It's worth the time you'll need to invest upfront to develop your editorial calendar. It will become the cornerstone of your communications routines.

CHAPTER 23

Create a Standard Creation, Review, and Approval Process

Getting great results from your communications work is often contingent on timing. It needs to get out the door or online quickly to be relevant.

But a painful review and approval process can cripple your creative work, no matter how good it is.

We've all been there . . .

- You missed a great opportunity to comment on breaking news and get your organization quoted in a major paper, because you couldn't get the talking points approved in time and that news cycle is now over.
- Endless wordsmithing of the appeal letter means that it's going out several weeks late, and now it's hitting at the same time you are supposed to be marketing a fundraising event instead.
- You had the perfect holiday story lined up, but program staff wavered about whether the subject of the story was really

the best client to highlight. Now the holiday has come and gone, and the story lacks the same emotional punch.

Creating a standard content creation, review, and approval process—and having the authority or sheer force of will to hold people to it—can go a long way in avoiding these situations.

After all, your communications will be stronger if they are produced in a collaborative way. But that collaboration demands a process with firm ground rules and the willingness of managers to participate.

A Self-Professed Control Freak Lets Go and Embraces a Collaborative Process

Julie Bornhoeft, the chief development and marketing officer for WEAVE in Sacramento, California, knew she was "being a control freak and overthinking content." By creating a new process for creating and reviewing content, she was able to let go, empower her team, and get better results.

Julie's team started by creating a simple editorial calendar for their monthly newsletter, with the article topics and who was responsible for each article. Once team members complete their drafts, everyone pitches in to edit each other's work, reviewing spelling, grammar, and overall content. This gives Julie the confidence that the final content is strong.

Once the content is approved the first time, usually as donor communications or newsletter articles, team members are empowered to adapt it for social media, the website, and other channels. Julie doesn't need to approve those repurposed pieces again. "I know that if someone on my team is uncertain of how to use or frame the content, they will ask," says Julie.

Because of this new collaborative process, the team more frequently discusses who content is for and where it can be repurposed. "One of the greatest benefits to being more collaborative as a team is that staff can say when a topic should be framed differently for other demographics they are familiar with, whether defined by age, culture, ethnicity, gender, etc.," says Julie.

"This process has streamlined content approval, made for more compelling content, and increased traffic to the website, because we update it more often," says Julie.

Julie admits it wasn't easy at first. She had to consciously work to stop micromanaging. "I realized that my team is a rock star group of individuals who can only excel if I get out of the way. Overthinking every decision was stifling them, denying them the chance to thrive, and to build their skill sets," says Julie. The results are even better than Julie expected. "We are far more efficient now, and I believe our content has more depth and variety. My team is more willing to challenge my ideas, which I think is critical to effective communications in support of our mission."

Thinking Through Key Decisions in Your Content Creation, Review, and Approval Process

Just how complicated your content creation, review, and approval process should be will depend on the type of content you are creating, how many people internally have a role to play with that content, and how much decision making has been entrusted to you.

Here's a menu of elements that you might want to include in your own review and approval process.

Use a Creative Brief to Get Buy-In at the Start. Start by discussing upfront and reaching agreement on what the content needs to accomplish. See Chapter 5 for the questions included in a creative brief.

Incorporate the Process into Meetings. End each meeting by summarizing what decisions were made and by reviewing assignments and deadlines. Ideally, you can type assignments and deadlines into a project management tool during the meeting.

Agree on a Limited Number of Review Rounds. Talk about what's reasonable before you start and make sure people understand how many times they get to see it and which round or cycle you are on. You might label a draft "Review Round 2 of 3" for example.

Discuss Decision Making Order to Avoid Last-Minute Grenades. Those last-minute great ideas and second-guessing at the end of the process can blow up your entire project. Be clear about what's going to be decided and when, and discourage backtracking. You can even tie these decisions to your review rounds. Make sure that people understand where you are in the process and at what stage their input is appropriate, and when it's simply too late. This can be difficult with an executive director who only wants sign-off at the end, for example. It's best to provide updates or check-ins as you go along to avoid any unpleasant surprises.

Assign and Limit Who Reviews for What. Not everyone in the office should get carte blanche editing rights. For example, you might tell your program staff to edit primarily for substantive content, but that you won't feel obligated to accept their wordsmithing. You might ask your executive director to edit for tone, and to trust that the program staff have the factual substance covered. You might ask another communications team member to proofread only for grammar and typos. Go back to the Collaboration chapters if you need a refresher on roles and responsibilities.

Set Reasonable Turnaround Times and Hold People to Them. The default should be that if someone doesn't meet a review deadline, the process moves on without their comments. Of course, things come up and you may occasionally need to push deadlines, but that should be the exception to the rule, not the standard procedure. If getting their feedback into a document is important to them, they need to make time to participate in the process, including meeting deadlines.

Agree on What's Good Enough. Don't let the perfect be the enemy of the good. Decide ahead of time which criteria are most important and in what order. For example, "typo-free" may be more important than "fast and timely," but "fast and timely" may be more important than including a great level of detail or using the absolute best example possible.

Save the Polishing Until the End. It makes no sense to labor over word choices, the order of different sentences, and the finer points of grammar and punctuation until the heart (the substance) and soul (the tone) of the piece are right. With the big bones in place, you can then noodle around with the smaller decisions, assuming you still have room in your timeline.

Identify the Final Decisionmaker. It's natural for you to receive lots of comments, and for those comments to be in conflict. We all know the perils of writing and designing by committee. Ultimately, one person needs to make the final decisions, using the creative brief as a guide. Everyone else should agree to disagree.

Who that person is should vary from project to project. It doesn't always need to be the person with the biggest title – they often don't have time to resolve these disputes! Who has the most invested in the success of the piece, or who will be using it the most, or who has the most expertise? Those questions, more than job title, will often lead you to your final decision maker.

Share the Final Product with Anyone Who Touched It. Don't forget to let everyone who was involved in the creation see the final result. This is a great time to publicly praise your coworkers' special contributions or compliance with the process.

Reality Check Your Process and Adjust as Needed. All of this may look great on paper, but human beings have a way of being difficult and complicated sometimes. Talk honestly about what worked and what didn't and make adjustments where you can.

As a communications director, it's your responsibility to develop and manage the content creation, review and approval process within your organization. If there's no real process in place right now, you may need to start with small steps to institutionalize some of these methods.

CHAPTER 24

Build an Office Culture That Respects Deadlines

It's a common frustration for nonprofit communications directors who are trying to work collaboratively with staff: getting people to meet their deadlines.

This is a hard first step, but one that's essential: if you want someone to meet your deadlines, they have to believe it's important to do so. And that means that they understand the strategic role of communications for your organization, and how great communications are essential to great programmatic and fundraising results. Without the buy-in, your job as deadline enforcer is much more difficult.

But even with that understanding, you'll still run into situations where people just don't cooperate.

As an example, let's use getting staff members to submit articles for a blog or newsletter. Here are some approaches you might try.

Methods for Enforcing Deadlines Across the Organization

Be very specific about the task and the deadline. Suggestions and deadlines are not the same things. If you say something like, "I'd love to have it by Friday," that's not a real deadline. "Submit a newsletter article by the end of the week" is still too vague. How many words do you need? What's the article's focus? Exactly what day and what time is it due?

Make deadlines—and whether they are met—public information in the office. Transparency breeds accountability. Make staff deadlines public, and state in a matter-of-fact way who met this month's deadlines and who didn't. Perhaps you could send a regular email that includes the contributor's name, topic, deadline, and when the article was actually submitted. You could even color code early, on-time, and late. You are simply reporting the facts, so what appears next to the person's name is entirely up to them.

Even if you don't go public, you need to have a private conversation with the person about the missed deadline. They need to know that you know they missed it, and that it's a problem for you. If you just ignore the missed deadline, it's a signal that it didn't really matter and they were right to prioritize something else over meeting your deadline.

Try some other carrots and sticks. What works will depend on your office culture, but play around with some different kinds of rewards (something as simple as kudos from you or the boss in the staff meeting) and sticks (like refusing to promote their programs on social media until they meet your newsletter or blog deadlines).

Take a cue from reality TV and build in some friendly competition for those carrots and sticks. Departments that are most compliant with meeting your deadlines and producing the best articles don't have to clean the break room for a month; the loser departments do.

Give staff a big head start with models to copy. You need that newsletter article, but your project coordinator is stumped about how to get started. How about giving them some basic templates to choose from? For example, you could give them an outline of a how-to article or a Top Five list. If you are asking them to write more of a narrative story, share a few past examples, breaking down exactly how the story is told, paragraph by paragraph. Or, you could provide a Q & A template for the writer to follow, where you provide the questions and they provide the answers.

Be explicit about consequences to the project or the organization. Odds are you have some flexibility, but you can't let people take advantage of that all the time. When people miss deadlines over and over—especially when it's the boss—it's important that you outline the trade-offs.

Maybe you won't have enough time to carefully proofread everything, or maybe the newsletter will publish without important information. Or you won't be giving your supporters enough time to respond to your call to action, which means lackluster results. Or you will look like flakes. Or your supporters will forget who you are and why the work matters.

Again, this is a much easier case to make when staff and managers already believe in the value of high-quality, consistent communications.

How to Provide Personal Support
to Staff in Meeting Deadlines

Want to go even further, and provide some personalized help to your staff contributors?

Break it down into smaller deadlines. Instead of saying "your blog post is due in six weeks," consider breaking that down into some intermediate deadlines that will help the person bite off a chunk at a time. Ask for the topic, then a headline, then teaser copy, then a first draft, and then a final draft. Some writers need to do the full piece before they can give you teasers or headlines, and that's fine too, but you might ask to see the first draft earlier in that case.

Ask for potential roadblocks when you make the assignment. When you are first setting a deadline, ask the writers if they can see anything on their schedules and to-do lists that would get in the way of completing the assignment. This is really just to prompt them to think about their own time management, and to agree with you ahead of time that they can, in fact, get the work done. You might suggest that they block out time to do the work.

Get to know their writing styles and where they get stuck. Part of your job as a communications director is to help coach other staff on communications tasks. Get to know your bloggers and their writing styles. Who has a hard time getting started? Who are the perfectionists who have a hard time saying something is done? Who works best from an outline? Who works best under deadline pressure? Rather than using a one-size-fits-all approach, customize the help and nudges you provide based on what each person needs.

Diane Hill, development and communications coordinator for United Community Ministries of Alexandria, Virginia says holding firm on deadlines does require a "tough love" approach. She shares this example: "Even though our after-school programs are a current focus for messaging, if the program staff have not provided photos or content in a timely matter, we cannot relax or extend publication deadlines," says Diane. "We have to move on with another story or program highlight."

She feels confident in using this approach because her team is so accommodating in other ways. For example, communications staff read the monthly reports of program staff first, before developing a list of questions. Communications staff also meet in person at least monthly with each program area, during their staff meetings, to share editorial calendar ideas and to collect program input for articles, client stories, and fundraising appeals. "In general, fundraising and communications staff bend over backwards to make it as easy as possible for program staff to share info with us," says Diane. "We also do a monthly 'call for content' for the agency e-newsletter. We collect future messaging ideas that way too."

The people you are communicating with expect timely content. The only way you can deliver on that expectation is with timely work products from your coworkers. Work through these methods to help build a culture that respects communications deadlines.

CHAPTER 25

Simplify Communications Routines So Others Can Follow Them

In the Agile section, we looked at some simple rules to help you make better, faster decisions. In their book, *Simple Rules: How to Thrive in a Complex World*, Sull and Eisenhardt also suggest several different kinds of simple rules related to processes, or how to do things better. They include How-To Rules, Timing Rules, and Coordination Rules.

These rules are especially important to create if you want help from others within your organization with communications responsibilities. They need to know how to do the work well without your constant hand-holding and review.

How-To Rules guide the basics of executing tasks. Think about formulas or step-by-step guidelines you could create for others to follow.

AARP's Rule of One for Facebook posts is a great example. It's a formula for posts that includes one photo, one sentence, one link, and one request from readers. They don't do it every single time, but if you scan their page, you'll see the formula a lot.

157

Timing Rules can specify that certain actions take place when triggering events happen. They can create deadlines, rhythms, and sequences to the work.

Implementing a process for adding items to your editorial calendar is one way to codify timing rules. For example, you could set a rule that all draft newsletter articles and blog posts must be submitted 48 hours before their publication time. You could set timing rules about event marketing: save the date cards are mailed eight weeks before the event, weekly reminders are sent in the month before the event, and daily reminders are sent in the last 72 hours before the event.

Coordination Rules explain how individuals should behave to produce a group result. This is what governs complex interactions in nature among flocks of birds and bees in a hive. Humans use coordination rules too! For example, in improvisational comedy, simple rules include not telling jokes, always making others look good, and building on what was just said with "Yes, and . . ." These rules are not about "when" like Timing Rules, but rather about "how."

Mandating participation in regular editorial meetings is a Coordination Rule. If program staff want their work included in the nonprofit's communications, they must attend the meetings where those decisions are discussed and made.

Think about opportunities to test run some of these simple rules, such as when you go on vacation or parental leave. These planned absences give everyone a heads-up that they'll be following the rules you have already created for them, and can serve as good practice for times when they'll need to fill in without as much notice.

CHAPTER 26

Improve Your Personal Productivity

It's tough to implement methods that keep your nonprofit marketing organized and on track when you can't effectively manage your own time, attention, and energy. There are many productivity methods out there, and I've tried quite a few myself.

I have two book recommendations for you.

Work Simply: Embracing the Power of Personal Productivity Style by Carson Tate helps you figure out what makes you tick. Are you a Planner, Prioritizer, Visualizer, or Arranger? Carson helps you figure out which of the four productivity styles best match your personal approach to work, and offers lots of tips on maximizing your own productivity and how to work well with other styles too.

How to Be a Productivity Ninja: Worry Less, Achieve More and Love What You Do by Graham Allcott is my favorite "systems" book and I use the methods in it (with some personal tweaks) to manage both my inbox and my to-do lists. The "CORD" approach in the book—Collect, Organize, Review, Do—has made a huge difference in managing all the information, requests, and ideas that come up every day.

If you aren't ready to dive into another productivity book, I will save you some time. I've compiled nine productivity tactics that have worked for me in some way or another and that I know have worked for other communications directors.

Try just one of the tactics below every day for at least two weeks. Do not (I repeat) **do not** try them all at once! The goal is to see if adopting a tactic and using it consistently, every day—making it a new habit— can have a significant impact on how you feel at work.

Option 1: Get Real about How You Spend Your Time

Not sure where all of your time really goes?

Find out what's really eating up your time, and how that matches up with your priorities by doing an honest time tracking assessment. For at least two weeks and ideally four, commit to detailed time tracking (in 10 or 15 minute increments) using a tool like Toggl.com, which is my personal favorite. You set up the various projects or types of tasks and log what you do and for how long. After a week or two, go back and review the totals. Are you spending your time on the right priorities?

Option 2: Set a Higher Standard for Getting on Your Calendar

Here's your goal: put fewer meetings or events on your calendar. Before you put a meeting on your schedule, run it through this question gauntlet:

- Do I personally need to be at this meeting? Can someone else do it? What specific value am I adding by being there? How will the meeting fail if I am not there?

- Does this meeting really need to take place? Do I really need to talk to this person? What happens if I don't?
- How long is enough time? What can we get done in 15 minutes? (Don't make meetings an hour by default!)
- Question the timing. Does this really need to be done NOW? What if it waits a day, a week, a month? (It's amazing how many "urgent" things shrink as priorities or take care of themselves with a little benign neglect.)

See how many meetings or other events you can avoid by applying these or other criteria.

Option 3: Try Calendar Time Blocking for Important Tasks – or Unimportant Ones

Calendar time blocking is where you move priorities from your to-do list into your calendar based on how long each task takes. You can also use it in reverse: to put limits on the amount of time you spend on things that have a way of eating up too much time, like meetings or email. Maybe you say you'll only spend 10 hours a week in meetings. When you reach the limit, no more meetings. Or maybe you'll only spend one hour in the morning and one in the afternoon on email. Schedule it and stick to it.

Option 4: Try Daily Themes or Calendar Chunking

This is different approach to your calendar. Instead of noting specific tasks or events in small blocks, block off bigger chunks or even whole days for certain kinds of tasks. For example, I block off Mondays for all of my administrative and planning work. If I am writing a book or series of blog posts, I know I work best in uninterrupted chunks of three-four hours.

Option 5: Adopt the Pomodoro Technique and Use It Daily

Focus on one thing and one thing only for 25 minutes at a time. Set a timer so you don't have to think about it. (The name Pomodoro comes from using a kitchen timer shaped like a tomato). After the 25 minutes, take a five-minute break. Then start again with another 25-minute work session.

Option 6: Turn Off All Notifications for Email and Social Media

On all of your computers and mobile devices, turn off the audio pings and visual cues about new messages. Instead, you decide how often and when you need to check them—whatever makes sense to you. Maybe that's once an hour or twice a day.

Warning: this is harder than it sounds! We've been conditioned to look for notifications and you'll likely go through withdrawal at first, frequently checking or reaching for your phone. Keep track of that! Are you able to break the cycle and get back in control of these tools, instead of the other way around?

Option 7: Cull Your To-Do List Back to "Next Action" Only

This is straight out of David Allen's "Getting Things Done" method. The idea is to focus exclusively on the next specific action step that needs to take place. You can have a separate project plan where ALL the steps associated with a project live, but only the next action that you must take goes on to your to-do list.

If you use project management or sophisticated list management software, one way to do this is to not assign a due date to anything but your next action step. Then you only look at items with due dates.

Option 8: Only Check and Respond to Email During Set Times

Treat your time in your inbox like a scheduled meeting on your calendar. Put it on your schedule for just once, twice, or at most, three times a day. Limit the amount of time at each sitting (30 minutes?). This is the only time you get in your inbox!

Think you might need information in your email for work during other times? Plan ahead and get it out of the email during one of your scheduled email sessions. If you absolutely must get into your email outside of your set time, get in and out fast, doing NOTHING ELSE but retrieving the information you need.

Option 9: Get to Inbox Zero By Using the Productivity Ninja Email Processing System

Don't treat your inbox like your to-do list. They aren't the same thing. Instead, create a system that helps you quickly get incoming email out of the inbox and into the right place. If you follow the system described in *How to Be a Productivity Ninja: Worry Less, Achieve More and Love What You Do*, with each message in your inbox, you process it this way:

- Can I delete it now? (and perhaps unsubscribe if you often delete the same thing).
- Can I archive it now? If no action now, but you might need it later, perhaps with some tagging.
- Can I delegate it now, by forwarding to someone else with directions?
- Can I do it now, if it will take less than two minutes?
- Everything else, move to a "live action" folder. *Productivity Ninja* recommends three folders: "ACTION" meaning you

need to do something; "READ" meaning information you want to review, but where no action of you is required; and "WAITING" where you are waiting on other people to take action. Within the Action folder, you might use additional tagging to help you identify the kind of task it is.

This system helps you empty the inbox quickly, leaving you time to focus on the live action folders.

Doing Less Can Help You Do More

While all of the tips in this chapter can be helpful with managing your calendar and to-do list, it's also important to keep the big picture in mind: rested minds and bodies are more creative and productive in the long-run.

Adam Nevins, executive director of ServLife International, Inc. in Indianapolis, Indiana, emphasizes this with his staff. The ServLife brand in based on the personal touch. "We don't just broadcast communications, we personally share. Our staff personally meets with over half our donor base over the course of a year," says Adam. To be effective at that, says Adam, his staff need a personal emotional capacity to do the work, and he sees growing that capacity as part of his responsibility as a leader. He encourages staff time for "unproductive solitude." "One day a month each staff member takes a personal day to read, hike, unplug," says Adam. "This has been transformative for us and has unlocked levels of creativity, and then collaboration, that have never existed before."

You are not a machine. You are complicated human being doing challenging work. Understanding your own productivity style, and implementing methods that support that, will help not only you, but your organization, thrive in this work.

PART 6

Use CALM
to Solve Common Challenges

If you've read this book straight through, you've worked through dozens of chapters, each with a different approach to being less BUSY and more CALM.

Of course, most of these individual solutions work best when used together in different combinations. Let's explore some of those combinations now.

In this section, you'll meet several people you will likely recognize, even though they are all fictional characters. Each situation is based on real experiences shared with me by nonprofit communications directors in the last few years.

After reading each story, take a few minutes to think about how you would suggest the character apply CALM principles to their situations. Then turn the page, and I'll share some of my ideas with you.

CHAPTER 27

She Has Too Many Tasks, But Little Authority

C arrie is a 24-year-old fundraising and communications coordinator at a large social services agency. She reports to the executive director, Alice, and has a good relationship with her.

Carrie is the first person to fill this job full-time, and it's her first professional job out of college. Everyone sees Carrie as catchall utility player. They are so relieved that someone else now has communications and fundraising responsibilities!

But that means new tasks get dumped in Carrie's lap daily, most with a great deal of urgency and very little planning. She's quickly feeling overwhelmed and unproductive. But she doesn't want to be seen as complaining, because everyone else is busy too!

What should Carrie do to improve this situation?

Jot down a few ideas of your own, then turn the page to hear my advice.

Kivi's Advice When You Have Too Many Tasks, But Little Authority

I recommend that Carrie **begin with a *Big Picture Communications Timeline* exercise** to help map out the communications needs for the organization as a whole. It's essential to get that bigger picture perspective when she feels bogged down by a million tasks. It's equally important for her coworkers to get that perspective on how their pieces fit into the bigger picture (see Chapter 4).

Next, Carrie should start working on an editorial calendar (see Chapter 22). In cases like this, I recommend that Carrie is explicit about the number of times she can reasonably communicate through the various communications channels, e.g. how many emails and Facebook posts can go out in a week? In addition to that, how much capacity does she have for one-off work, like creating flyers for coworkers? Build the calendar out as a series of empty blocks that can be filled with requests. When the blocks are filled, and a new, more important request comes in, something in a block now gets bumped out, rather than just heaped onto the pile.

Because there's much more work than she can handle, and the editorial calendar will only have so many blocks that can be filled, Carrie should also work on a **system for managing all the good ideas and non-urgent requests that she gets** (see Chapter 6). Even if she can't do the work now, she can put the idea or request in some kind of holding pen.

Learning how to gracefully but clearly say "no" is another skill that Carrie should develop (see Chapter 19). This is a tough one, particularly for less experienced and people-pleasing personalities. But it's an important skill to develop, not only to maintain personal productivity and happiness at work, but to keep the nonprofit focused on its priorities.

Finally, over the long-term, I recommend that Carrie **develop a standard review process** (see Chapter 23). This will help ensure that other staff appreciate all the steps involved in creating good communications and the need to budget for that time. Coupled with the editorial calendar, it will help Carrie better manage her workflow if she knows which communications pieces are at what point in the review process.

CHAPTER 28

He Was Promoted from Tactical Worker to Strategic Leader

Juan is a 30-year-old communications director working at a nonprofit that offers classes in visual and performing arts. He started there as a part-time graphic designer a couple of years ago and was promoted internally to the communications director role when the last person left.

He is confident in his design skills, but is beginning to understand that this job is going to require that he stretch himself as he grows into the job. His only concern previously was creating content at the direction of others. Now he's the one who is supposed to be thinking strategically about messaging and editorial planning. He's been a participant in those meetings before, but never led them.

Where should Juan begin?

Jot down a few ideas of your own, then turn the page to hear my advice.

Kivi's Advice When You Need to Move from Tactical Thinking to Strategic Leadership

It's time for Juan to take charge (see Chapter 13). He's in a leadership role now, and needs to fully assume that responsibility.

To make good decisions, Juan should dedicate some time to better understanding the needs of the organization as a whole and **opening lines of internal communications with coworkers** (see Chapter 5). I recommend that he devote time to meeting with each of his coworkers and listening to their needs and their thoughts on his new role.

These conversations should also include discussions on the priority goals of other departments. As a leader, it's part of Juan's job **to both limit and integrate communications goals with other organizational goals** (see Chapter 17).

To give himself some confidence and time to grow into the new role, I recommend that he study **communications and fundraising best practices, and use those as the starting point** for decision making (see Chapter 20). After playing it safe and building some confidence as a leader, he can start to build in some experimentation.

Over the long-term, I'd remind Juan to always **expect the unexpected** (see Chapter 15) and to do his best to prepare for both opportunities and crises that could affect his team.

CHAPTER 29

She Wants to Stop Reacting and Get More Strategic

Janelle is a 48-year-old communications director who's worked at a few different nonprofits in her career. She manages two junior staff who focus on content creation and community engagement, in support of both fundraising and policy advocacy, which are often linked. Her team is competent and trusted by management, but she knows both she and her staff are trying to do too much.

New opportunities are constantly coming up, and she feels like they react to what's new all the time. She would really like to be more strategic and more systematic in the work.

Janelle also sees the potential for her team to grow, but she wants that growth to be thoughtful and organized so that the nonprofit's resources are used for the greatest good.

How can Janelle and her team be more strategic?

Jot down a few ideas of your own, then turn the page to hear my advice.

Kivi's Advice When You Want to Be Less Reactive and More Strategic

First and foremost, Janelle needs to be crystal clear about what those strategic goals are. **Limiting and integrating her team's goals** with larger organizational goals is essential (see Chapter 17).

My next several recommendations are all ways to filter everything else that comes up so that Janelle and her team react appropriately. After all, you can't really stop all of the ideas and requests, but you can control how you react to them and what you do with them in both the short term and long term.

When Janelle finds that most of her time is spent reacting rather than working proactively on strategic priorities, there's a breakdown in the way she is making decisions about her time and energy. Rather than automatically giving her time to the loudest, or newest and most exciting, or most urgent requests by coworkers, how does she make decisions that allow the quieter but more important and strategic work to get what it deserves?

I'd encourage Janelle to take a closer look at decision making within her team and the larger organization. **How should decisions be made** to protect those strategic goals (see Chapter 8)? How can her team **make good decisions more quickly** (see Chapter 14)?

Coupled with better decision making comes better preparedness. Rather than being caught off guard and having to react to both great opportunities and crises, Janelle can **spend some time planning for the unexpected** (see Chapter 15).

Finally, I'd encourage Janelle to **explore tools to improve her team's efficiency** (see Chapter 26). Much of the hurried and harried feelings that communications teams feel can be smoothed, at least partially, with better productivity and communications tools.

CHAPTER 30

Her Boss Won't Delegate

Heather is a 50-year-old manager of fundraising and communications. She reports to Sherry, the 62-year-old VP of development, who mostly manages major donors, and corporate and foundation relations. Sherry leaves smaller donors and the organization's broader community engagement and brand communications to Heather and her small team – at least in theory.

However, whenever Heather tries to do anything different at all, Sherry balks. Sherry is risk averse and doesn't want anything Heather might do to negatively influence her major gifts. She doesn't really understand integrated communications channels like direct mail, email, and social media campaigns, and admits that.

Heather knows she and her team could do great work if she could just get Sherry to let her.

What should Heather do?

Jot down a few ideas of your own, then turn the page to hear my advice.

175

Kivi's Advice When Your Supervisor Won't Delegate

Heather's challenge is to build trust and credibility with her boss on a personal level and in her team, while also instilling some accountability on Sherry's part to work with her to meet the organization's goals in the long term.

I'd suggest that Heather first look at ways to shore up Sherry's **trust in both her competence** (see Chapter 11) and **her intentions** (see Chapter 12), and then to do the same with her team members. Sherry lets Heather do the work, as long as it fits within Sherry's comfort zone. To move beyond that, Heather should first reinforce that she does, in fact, know what she is doing and that her intent is to help both Sherry and the nonprofit succeed.

Next, Heather should work on **connecting the dots** between the new things she wants to try and the mutual goals that she and Sherry are responsible for (see Chapter 4). It needs to be clear that these are not wacky ideas, but modern and accepted approaches to the work that Heather's team has been asked to do.

Creating a clear review process (see Chapter 23) so that Sherry can be brought along slowly is a good next step. Heather can reassure her that she won't be caught by surprise because Heather will commit to that process and keep her in the loop.

This goes hand in hand with working to **build a better culture around deadlines** within the team (see Chapter 24). If Sherry agrees to the process and deadlines in advance, Heather can hopefully use that as additional leverage when Sherry balks or delays.

Finally, it wouldn't hurt for Heather to **brush up on some conflict resolution skills** to help work through the more challenging conversations with Sherry (see Chapter 9).

CHAPTER 31

She's Trying to Make Big Changes, But Coworkers Won't Budge

Janice is a 32-year-old recently hired communications director. This is her first director-level position, after many years as a communications coordinator.

The position was vacant for over a year, so Janice has a long list of things that need attention.

But the message she is getting from program staff and other managers is "not so fast!" Every time she suggests overhauling the website or launching a new newsletter, she gets lots of pushback and "devil's advocate" responses about why the timing is bad and how much work it will create, with uncertain gains.

Everyone gets along personally, and no one is fully dismissive of her suggestions, yet very few of her ideas are gaining traction.

What should Janice do?

Jot down a few ideas of your own, then turn the page to hear my advice.

Kivi's Advice When Coworkers Don't Embrace Your Big Plans

Janice's case is a classic example of where nonprofit consensus culture can get in the way of making important and much-needed changes.

I'd encourage Janice to focus on two aspects: decision making and accountability. Someone has to be responsible for communications progress, and that someone should be her as the communications director. With that responsibility comes an obligation to listen to others and to seek good, workable solutions when legitimate concerns are raised. But communications work frequently involves hard choices and trade-offs. That's where the accountability comes in.

I'd suggest Janice **openly talk about how decisions are made** in the organization, especially with respect to the work load she manages (see Chapter 8). What should she be empowered to decide after consultation and what needs full buy-in from others?

At the same time, she should **open conversations about team accountability**: her accountability to the organization's goals, accountability to her coworkers, and their accountability to her in helping her succeed (see Chapter 7). Even though projects like website overhauls are difficult and time-consuming, they are necessary and communications teams need to find ways to make them happen.

Next, I would encourage Janice to look at **how she can make decisions that are within her control** (or should be) much faster (see Chapter 14), freeing up more time and focus for discussions on issues that do require more group work.

Lastly, to help Janice stay inspired, she should **experiment wherever she can** (see Chapter 20) and **celebrate what progress she does make every day**, even when those wins seem small (see Chapter 21).

CHAPTER 32

He's Working Too Much, But Can't Let Go

Allen, a 42-year-old communications director, has always been a perfectionist. He prides himself on being very responsible and diligent. His organization has an ambitious communications plan, and he wants to do it all and do it right.

But he's getting bogged down. He's starting to miss deadlines, and that's really stressing him out. He's working after hours more often, and it's negatively affecting his family life. To compensate, he's started skipping lunch and working secretly at home when he doesn't think his partner and kids are looking.

One day, he pretended to take a shower when he was really in the bathroom responding to emails. When his daughter complained through the closed door that he was using all the hot water, and he realized that he wasn't even in the shower, he knew something had to change.

Where should Allen start?

Jot down a few ideas of your own, then turn the page to hear my advice.

Kivi's Advice When Your Dedication to Your Work Takes Over Your Life

We all know that acknowledging a problem is the first step toward solving it, but that next step can be very difficult to discern sometimes!

Allen's situation is the culmination of several problems, which means that a long-term solution will be multi-faceted too.

From the organizational side, Allen needs to **get some clarity on what's truly a priority** (see Chapter 18). The differences between must-dos, really important tasks, and nice-to-haves are often difficult to see when you are stuck deep in a project, but those differences do exist in any project.

Allen can also change up his approach to the work itself. I'd encourage him to figure out ways to **simplify common routines** (see Chapter 25) and to **focus on creating agile content** that can be repurposed easily (see Chapter 16). When communications directors are overworked, there's often too much custom work and "reinvention of the wheel" taking place. Streamlining those processes and workflows can free up quite a bit of time.

Allen can also take a **look at his own personal productivity and work habits** (see Chapter 26). Simple changes in how you respond to interruptions, and resetting expectations about response times to inputs like email, can make a big difference.

Finally, Allen, like all perfectionists, needs to **learn how to say "no" not only to others, but to himself** and to be satisfied with "good" work rather than always expecting "perfect" from himself and others.

CHAPTER 33

Her Visionary Boss is Making Her Miserable

Sheila is a 44-year-old communications director who reports directly to Lynn, the founder of an animal sanctuary.

Lynn is a true visionary who founded the organization more than 30 years ago. She's been saying that she will retire next year for about the last ten years. She's also not much of a people person, preferring to spend her time with the animals they rescue. She comes up with lots of great ideas while she's walking among the animals.

To put it simply, Sheila is getting tired of working for Lynn. Last week's urgent priority is always replaced with a new one the following week. Sheila feels like she never gets to finish anything. Lynn has unrealistic expectations for how long things take to get done, and she occasionally berates Sheila for not being able to keep up.

Sheila loves the organization and needs this job. What can Sheila do to improve her work life?

Jot down a few ideas of your own, then turn the page to hear my advice.

Kivi's Advice When Your Visionary Boss is Making You Miserable

Some bosses are simply difficult people to work for, and visionaries in particular are nearly impossible to change. But if Sheila loves the job, I do have several suggestions for her.

First and foremost, Sheila has to **take responsibility for improving the working relationship** (see Chapter 10). Lynn isn't going to get a personality transplant.

Asking for guidance on priorities is always worth a try (see Chapter 18), but in cases like these, those priorities change so often that forcing those conversations may not be that helpful.

I would, however, encourage Sheila to stand up for herself in conversations with Lynn about what she needs in order to do her best work for the animals. Building Lynn's **trust in her intentions**—to do the best work for the animals as Lynn does—is essential (see Chapter 12), followed by **trust in her competence** (see Chapter 11).

At the most practical level, Sheila needs to **work on managing what she hears** from Lynn (see Chapter 6) and figuring out her own responses. Just how far should she go with certain ideas before waiting to see if they are lasting and important to Lynn? Where should she regularly demonstrate and highlight progress? What can she leave on the back burner, perhaps indefinitely?

Being extremely agile with content creation (see Chapter 16) is also a great skill to develop when working for someone who changes her mind frequently. When you start to create content that is scrapped in the middle of your process, don't archive it away forever. Keep it handy, labeled in a way that reminds you what you accomplished. Use it a first draft for another project.

CHAPTER 34

She is Doing the Work of Three People

Ryan is a 27-year-old communications coordinator. When she joined her nonprofit two years ago, she reported to the communications director, and the team also included a database manager. About three months ago, both of those people left the organization for new positions elsewhere.

Ryan was asked to keep things moving along while the executive director and board talked about whether and how to fill the positions. There was talk of a re-organization because they recently finished a new strategic plan and they thought a different staffing structure could better support the plan.

But there doesn't seem to be any urgency about deciding on that structure or hiring. Meanwhile, Ryan is doing the work of three people. It's wearing her out. She's asked when the positions will be advertised several times, but doesn't get a straight answer.

What should Ryan do?

Jot down a few ideas of your own, then turn the page to hear my advice.

Kivi's Advice When You Are Doing the Work of Three People and Promised Help is Nowhere in Sight

It's no surprise that competent people tend to get more work assigned to them. When Ryan decided to be a good team player while the organization was in a staffing pinch, her managers may have seen that as an indication that they could get the same work done with fewer staff. Look, Ryan *can* handle it all!

Ryan needs to quickly quash this idea, just in case it's behind the hiring procrastination. My suggested approach is a combination of **taking charge of the situation** (see Chapter 13) and **saying "no"** to new work, and even to currently assigned responsibilities (see Chapter 19). Re-organizations and hiring are hard and time-consuming—and therefore easy to avoid as long as you can. Ryan needs to convey that time is up on this arrangement. This may come as shock to the system for everyone involved, including Ryan, but it has to be done.

In the short-term, Ryan should also triage the workload. She simply can't do it all. So **what processes can be simplified**, perhaps even so others in the office could pick them up (see Chapter 25)?

Ryan should also **look at her own personal productivity**, not with an eye toward doing more, but with the goal of better managing her own energy and sanity (see Chapter 26). What working accommodations can she ask for until more staff are hired (e.g. coming in later or working from home)?

Ultimately, this is about **holding the management team accountable** for their staffing responsibilities. Ryan can use some of the suggestions around team accountability for this purpose as well (see Chapter 7).

CHAPTER 35

Everyone's So Busy, She Gets No Help with Content

Ellen is a 26-year-old communications coordinator who manages a science and technology organization's blog, newsletters, and social media. Most of the staff are highly trained and experienced scientists and engineers.

Ellen is a self-professed geek, but writing and editing are her strong suits, not the complex scientific and engineering processes that the technical staff live and breathe.

The technical staff are supposed to give her content regularly, but they rarely do. She only gets what she needs on their terms, when they feel like it.

As a result, there's no rhyme or reason to what Ellen is publishing through their communications channels. She never really knows what she'll get until it lands in her inbox.

What should Ellen do?

Jot down a few ideas of your own, then turn the page to hear my advice.

Kivi's Advice on Getting Help
with Content from Busy People

Ellen's predicament isn't confined to technical fields. Nonprofit staff of all walks of life are too busy or too focused on their own work to pay much attention to the needs of communications staff.

My first recommendation to Ellen is to **establish an editorial calendar** (see Chapter 22) and to bring it with her everywhere she goes, and to make it as visible to others as humanly possible.

The next step is **building a culture that values meeting deadlines** (see Chapter 24) in that editorial calendar. This is a big culture shift for an organization like Ellen's. Top-down management support and clear expectations for technical staff would be ideal but Ellen may need to continue to use some of her begging and bartering skills for awhile. People love attention for their work, and Ellen can leverage the attention she can garner through good communications to motivate staff to be more cooperative.

Creating a standard review process (see Chapter 23) is a logical next step. If staff know for a fact that she will be publishing about their projects on a certain date because they now trust the editorial calendar and Ellen's commitment to deadlines, they are more likely to cooperate because they'll want their work to be described correctly. That means working with Ellen in the review process she has created.

But given the current culture, it's also wise for Ellen to **expect the unexpected** (see Chapter 15) and to prepare to fill gaps and changes in the editorial calendar regularly. Being extremely **agile with the content she does have** will also help immensely (see Chapter 16).

PART 7

How to Supervise
a Communications Team for CALM

Research by Nonprofit Marketing Guide in the 2016 and
2017 *Nonprofit Communications Trends Reports* confirms how
important strong relationships between executive directors and
communications directors are for both personal happiness at work
and organizational communications success.

I'll share some advice for how to manage a communication
team in the next chapter, but first some words of caution.

Specific behaviors on the part of managers can drain staff
motivation and put a huge dent in their sense of progress. Teresa
Amabile, a professor at Harvard Business School and author of *The
Progress Principle: Using Small Wins to Ignite Joy, Engagement, and
Creativity at Work,* identified four ways that managers routinely,
and probably unwittingly, zap the meaning out of their employees'
work. Three of these four are definite problems in the nonprofit
sector.

1. Dismissing the importance of employees' work or ideas and settling for mediocrity.

This is a big one for nonprofit communicators who work in organizations that don't value the strategic importance of good communications. If your nonprofit doesn't believe in and invest in the power of great communications to achieve its goals, it's hard to see how you can stay motivated for long.

2. Destroying a sense of ownership by switching people off project teams before work is finalized.

I don't see this happen quite as often in the nonprofit world, probably because nonprofits are chronically understaffed, so it's rare for people to get pulled off work. It's much more likely that new work gets piled on before the old work gets done – which leads us to problem #3.

3. Shifting goals so frequently that people despair that their work will ever see the light of day.

Bingo! No clear goals and shifting goals are a huge problem, especially in nonprofit communications where there are so many choices to be made each day. Unfortunately, many nonprofit managers focus too much on just producing communications without being clear about their goals for those communications.

4. Neglecting to keep staff up to date on changing priorities for customers.

Being kept out of the loop is another common complaint from communications directors, although the changing priorities are more likely to come from management than from a nonprofit's customers or clients. Keeping the internal lines of communication open is essential to keeping employees engaged.

CHAPTER 36

How Executive Directors Can Use the Four D's to Manage Teams for CALM

According to the *2016 Nonprofit Communications Trends Report*, about 48 percent of communications directors plan to leave their current position in the next two years. This mirrors the alarming rate of turnover among fundraisers documented in the landmark 2013 report *UnderDeveloped: A National Study of Challenges Facing Nonprofit Fundraising*, a joint project of CompassPoint and the Evelyn and Walter Haas, Jr. Fund.

What's driving this trend?

For many communications professionals who are looking to jump ship, the issues are clear.

Forty percent of the communications directors said that lack of management direction is a severe problem: about 22 percent complained about excessive management oversight.

As someone who works closely with communications professionals across the country, I'm not surprised by these concerns.

Chances are, your communications staff is feeling squeezed by several factors within your control. Lack of clear strategy and competing priorities are a huge problem for many nonprofits. And because there are so many different communications channels to manage, many communications professionals feel like they are on a treadmill, running fast but getting nowhere.

Often, they are being pulled in too many directions, with too many varied responsibilities, too many "bright ideas" being thrown at them by their executive directors, and not enough time to execute any of them.

As a result, they are frustrated – and looking elsewhere. Like many who work in the nonprofit world, communications directors want to make a difference, and they will gladly move on to an organization that will help them achieve more.

So how can you create an organization that is a prime landing spot for the best communications talent? Here are four practices—the four D's—that will help you more effectively work with and lead your communications team.

Dedicate time and resources. At many organizations, communications directors are not part of the senior management team. As a result, they are often not participating in or thinking about key organizational decisions until too late in the process.

If your nonprofit is serious about conveying the right message about your work and communicating effectively with your supporters, board members, and partners, stop treating your communications director like a short-order cook and add them to your senior team.

Regardless of your formal management structure, it's your responsibility to discuss openly ways to improve internal communications and foster cooperation among program, development, and communications staff. Our research shows that integrated communications and fundraising teams are likely to feel a greater sense of responsibility for accomplishing your goals and gain more satisfaction on the job.

Communications isn't a "nice to have" option. It is a discipline that is crucial to your nonprofit's success. By integrating your teams and giving communications staff a seat at the table, you ensure that those employees have a say in key decisions from the start, which will produce much better results in the end.

Define the work. Many of the biggest challenges facing communications leaders come from being asked to do too many things. The most effective organizations are adept at setting a few big goals and sticking to them. As a leader, it's important that you lead the process of making choices about your priorities.

What's more, you have the power to decide the scope of what your communications team should focus on. Some communications directors are assigned office-wide tech-support responsibilities because they are savvy computer and internet users. In other organizations, they are saddled with administrative tasks by executive directors who consider writing up board meeting minutes and proofreading grant reports to be "communications."

Assignments like these take time and focus away from the real job of communicating with the people who support your organization and influencing others to do so.

Delegate the work. Empower your communications staff to make decisions and put them into effect. Be clear about what you are delegating fully, where you should be consulted, and where you want to make final decisions.

As you delegate, allow staff to invest in learning about their profession and listen to what they learn! Nonprofit communications, marketing, and fundraising staff have access to bloggers who share abundantly, in addition to paid professional development programs.

But time and again, we see executive directors ruin great work by staff. It happens most often when a leader's personal preferences (and often ignorance of what works best) trump what's right for the actual target of the communications. Remember, you are not the target audience for your nonprofit's communications.

Allow communications staff to control their own time and calendars, and let them say no to you. They are constantly pulled into meetings and asked to do work that is distracting. Don't expect them to be "always on and available" to you, just because their work is all about communicating.

Discuss the work often. Many of the most effective nonprofit communications operations include executive directors who are actively engaged in talking with staff and who provide feedback at the right times. How can you ensure that you're engaging in the most productive way?

It starts by participating in regularly scheduled editorial meetings so you can be aware of what's happening and help ensure that your communications team work is in line with your organization's priorities.

Many smart executive directors also make time for check-in discussions as staff develop campaigns. They use these check-ins to be a flexible sounding board, asking questions and gaining insight into what the communications team is thinking. In these discussions, it's important to be explicit about when you are simply sharing your opinions and ideas, and when you are giving direction that staff must follow.

What else do you need to know to manage effectively and retain your communications staff members? Ask them. Odds are they'll echo much of what I've shared with you and add words of wisdom specific to your organization. If you want great communications to come out of your organization, start by communicating well within it.

Conclusion

At Nonprofit Marketing Guide, our motto is "Helping Communications Directors Learn the Job *and* Love the Job." The learning part is easy; the loving part can be a real challenge when your organization is more BUSY than CALM.

In this book, I hope you've discovered many different ways that you can bring more CALM to your own work life and to your nonprofit's approach to communications.

I want to leave you with an inspirational quote not from some famous dead person, but from a communications director, just like you. Here's the advice of Tracy Hutchinson Wallace, the communications officer for Habitat for Humanity Trinidad and Tobago in San Juan:

"Play the hand you were dealt and always play to your strengths. Coming from a strong bridge-playing background, my parents taught me at a very young age to not stress about the cards you don't get, but figure out how to use your hand to support your partner. Look for the opportunities."

Be CALM, play hard, have fun, and love the job.

References

Chapter 1

Crabbe, Tony. 2015. *Busy: How to Thrive in a World of Too Much.* Grand Central Publishing.

Nonprofit Marketing Guide, LLC. 2016. *Nonprofit Communications Trends Report.*

Chapter 3

Nonprofit Marketing Guide, LLC. 2017. *Nonprofit Communications Trends Report.*

Part 2 Introduction

Lencioni, Patrick. 2002. *The Five Dysfunctions of a Team: A Leadership Fable.* Jossey-Bass.

Chapter 4

Leroux Miller, Kivi. 2013. "Worksheet: Your Big Picture Communications Timeline," *Kivi's Nonprofit Communications Blog.* September 25 2013. http://www.nonprofitmarketingguide. com/blog/2013/09/25/worksheet-your-big-picture-communications-timeline/

Diane Hill, message to author via Nonprofit Marketing Guide's "Stories for Kivi's CALM not BUSY Book" online form, March 2017.

Chapter 5

Jeanine Marlow, message to author via Nonprofit Marketing Guide's "Stories for Kivi's CALM not BUSY Book" online form, March 2017.

Cheryl Mergurdichian, message to author via Nonprofit Marketing Guide's "Stories for Kivi's CALM not BUSY Book" online form, March 2017.

Chapter 6

Vallie Edenbo, message to author via Nonprofit Marketing Guide's "Stories for Kivi's CALM not BUSY Book" online form, March 2017.

Tracy Hutchinson Wallace, message to author via Nonprofit Marketing Guide's "Stories for Kivi's CALM not BUSY Book" online form, March 2017.

Nita Wilkinson, message to author via Nonprofit Marketing Guide's "Stories for Kivi's CALM not BUSY Book" online form, March 2017.

Diane Hill, message to author via Nonprofit Marketing Guide's "Stories for Kivi's CALM not BUSY Book" online form, March 2017.

Chapter 7

Wikipedia, Wikipedia's entry on the RACI Matrix. https://en.wikipedia.org/wiki/Responsibility_assignment_matrix

Julie Bornhoeft, message to author via Nonprofit Marketing Guide's "Stories for Kivi's CALM not BUSY Book" online form, March 2017.

Scarlett Bauman, message to author via Nonprofit Marketing Guide's "Stories for Kivi's CALM not BUSY Book" online form, March 2017.

Julie Edwards, message to author via Nonprofit Marketing Guide's "Stories for Kivi's CALM not BUSY Book" online form, March 2017.

Tracy Hutchinson Wallace, message to author via Nonprofit Marketing Guide's "Stories for Kivi's CALM not BUSY Book" online form, March 2017.

Tara Collins, message to author via Nonprofit Marketing Guide's "Stories for Kivi's CALM not BUSY Book" online form, March 2017.

Chapter 8

Lencioni, Patrick. 2002. *The Five Dysfunctions of a Team: A Leadership Fable.* Jossey-Bass.

Godin, Seth. Quote reported in *Consensus vs. Collaboration* by Marty Cagan, January 30, 2011. https://svpg.com/consensus-vs-collaboration/

Bezos, Jeff. *2016 Letter to Shareholders.* April 12, 2017. https://www.amazon.com/p/feature/z6o9g6sysxur57t

Chapter 9

Packard, Caroline C. 2015. "Resolving Conflict in Nonprofits," Yale Nonprofit Alliance. http://yalenonprofitalliance.org/wp-content/uploads/2015/08/Packard-Resolving-Conflict-in-Nonprofits-Article.pdf

Packard, Caroline C. 2015. "Lecture: "Mediation and Conflict Resolution in Nonprofits." Yale Nonprofit Alliance. http://yalenonprofitalliance.org/wp-content/uploads/2015/08/Slidedeck-Handout-Conflict-Resolution-in-Nonprofits.pdf

Neitlich, Andrew. *Coach Master Toolkit.* ATN Associates LLC. http://centerforexecutivecoaching.com/cmt/

Part 3 Introduction

Nonprofit Marketing Guide, LLC. 2016. *Nonprofit Communications Trends Report.*

Nonprofit Marketing Guide, LLC. 2017. *Nonprofit Communications Trends Report.*

Chapter 10

Hurwitz, Marc and Hurwitz, Samantha. 2015. *Leadership is Half the Story: A Fresh Look at Followership, Leadership and Collaboration.* Rotman-UTP Publishing.

Marcie Timmerman, message to author via Nonprofit Marketing Guide's "Stories for Kivi's CALM not BUSY Book" online form, March 2017.

Neitlich, Andrew. *Coach Master Toolkit.* ATN Associates LLC. http://centerforexecutivecoaching.com/cmt/

Chapter 11

Hill, Linda and Linebeck, Kent, 2012. "To Build Trust, Competence is Key." *Harvard Business Review.* https://hbr.org/2012/03/to-build-trust-competence-is-k

Hill, Linda and Linebeck, Kent, 2012. "For People to Trust You, Reveal Your Intentions." *Harvard Business Review.* https://hbr.org/2012/04/for-people-to-trust-you-reveal

Chapter 12

Hill, Linda and Linebeck, Kent. 2011. *Being the Boss: The 3 Imperatives for Becoming a Great Leader.* Harvard Business Review.

Hill, Linda and Linebeck, Kent, 2012. "To Build Trust, Competence is Key." *Harvard Business Review.* https://hbr.org/2012/03/to-build-trust-competence-is-k

Hill, Linda and Linebeck, Kent, 2012. "For People to Trust You, Reveal Your Intentions." *Harvard Business Review.* https://hbr.org/2012/04/for-people-to-trust-you-reveal

Chapter 13

Neitlich, Andrew. *Coach Master Toolkit.* ATN Associates LLC. http://centerforexecutivecoaching.com/cmt/

Chapter 14

Tierney, John. 2011. "Do You Suffer from Decision Fatigue?" *The New York Times Magazine.* August 21, 2011. http://www.nytimes.

com/2011/08/21/magazine/do-you-suffer-from-decision-fatigue.
html

Sull, Donald and Eisenhardt, Kathleen M. 2016. *Simple Rules:
How to Thrive in a Complex World.* Mariner Books.

Chapter 15

Gray, David, and Brown, Sunni, and Macanufo, James. 2010.
*Gamestorming: A Playbook for Innovators, Rulebreakers, and
Changemakers.* O'Reilly Media.

Chapter 17

Hammonds, Keith. "Michael Porter's Big Ideas." *Fast Company.*
February 28, 2001. https://www.fastcompany.com/42485/
michael-porters-big-ideas

Nonprofit Marketing Guide, LLC. 2017. *Nonprofit
Communications Trends Report.*

Chapter 18

Megan Bourque-Stith, message to author via Nonprofit
Marketing Guide's "Stories for Kivi's CALM not BUSY Book"
online form, March 2017.

Chapter 21

Amabile, Teresa and Kramer, Steven J. "The Power of Small
Wins." *Harvard Business Review.* May 2011.
https://hbr.org/2011/05/the-power-of-small-wins

Brian Olson, message to author via Nonprofit Marketing Guide's
"Stories for Kivi's CALM not BUSY Book" online form, March 2017.

Chapter 22

Sharp, Sharon. "How to Get Program Staff to Use Your Editorial
Calendar." *Kivi's Nonprofit Communications Blog.* July 18, 2017.

Chapter 23

Julie Bornhoeft, message to author via Nonprofit Marketing
Guide's "Stories for Kivi's CALM not BUSY Book" online form,
March 2017.

Chapter 24

Diane Hill, message to author via Nonprofit Marketing Guide's "Stories for Kivi's CALM not BUSY Book" online form, March 2017.

Chapter 25

Sull, Donald and Eisenhardt, Kathleen M. 2016. *Simple Rules: How to Thrive in a Complex World*. Mariner Books.

Leroux Miller, Kivi. "AARP's Rule of One for Facebook." Kivi's Nonprofit Communications Blog. December 2, 2014. http://www.nonprofitmarketingguide.com/blog/2014/12/03/aarps-rule-of-one-for-facebook/

Chapter 26

Tate, Carson. 2015. *Work Simply: Embracing the Power of Your Personal Productivity Style*. Portfolio.

Allcott, Graham. 2015. *How to be a Productivity Ninja: Worry Less, Achieve More and Love What You Do*. Icon Books.

Wikipedia, Wikipedia's entry on the Pomodoro Technique. https://en.wikipedia.org/wiki/Pomodoro_Technique

Allen, David. 2001. *Getting Things Done: The Art of Stress-Free Productivity*. Penguin Books.

Adam Nevins, message to author via Nonprofit Marketing Guide's "Stories for Kivi's CALM not BUSY Book" online form, March 2017.

Part 7 Introduction

Amabile, Teresa and Kramer, Steven. 2012. "How Leaders Kill Meaning at Work." *McKinsey and Company*. January 2012. http://www.mckinsey.com/global-themes/leadership/how-leaders-kill-meaning-at-work

Amabile, Teresa and Kramer, Steven J. "The Power of Small Wins." *Harvard Business Review*. May 2011. https://hbr.org/2011/05/the-power-of-small-wins

Chapter 36

Nonprofit Marketing Guide, LLC. 2016. *Nonprofit Communications Trends Report.*

Bell, Jeanine and Cornelius, Marla. 2013. *"UnderDeveloped: A National Study of Challenges Facing Nonprofit Fundraising."* Compasspoint. https://www.compasspoint.org/underdeveloped

Conclusion

Tracy Hutchinson Wallace, message to author via Nonprofit Marketing Guide's "Stories for Kivi's CALM not BUSY Book" online form, March 2017.

CPSIA information can be obtained
at www.ICGtesting.com
Printed in the USA
LVHW041619171218
600776LV00037B/1700/P